Praise for the First Edition of
Oakland Hills, Milwaukee Rivers

"Honest, raw, gritty, and inviting. Dr. Alford paints a descriptive picture of a life filled with ups, downs, successes, and regrets. I couldn't, and didn't, put it down."

— Craig W., Amazon Review

"This book made me laugh and cry. I could visualize every part of the story. Great work, Dr. Alford—can't wait for the next one!"

— Viranea M., Amazon Review

"A compelling story that resonates deeply with your life, challenges your thinking, and inspires you to be better. This was exactly what I needed."

— Paul B., Amazon Review

"After reading this book, I have a new respect for those who share their history and roots. It keeps you grounded until the very end."

— Davell E., Amazon Review

"If you're on a journey and need motivation, I highly recommend this book. Super great read from Dr. Key."

— Timothy L., Amazon Review

"A must-read in 2025! Highlights identity, belonging, and real-life relationship dynamics in a way that's reflective and bold."

— Tyron H., Amazon Review

"This book changed my perspective. It opened my eyes to be more patient and understanding. A must-read."

— Amazon Customer

OAKLAND HILLS MILWAUKEE RIVERS

—— A MEMOIR OF ——
SURVIVAL, IDENTITY,
AND PURPOSE

OAKLAND HILLS MILWAUKEE RIVERS

—A MEMOIR OF— SURVIVAL, IDENTITY, AND PURPOSE

KEYIMANI ALFORD

KEYWORDS
UNLOCKED

Copyright © 2025 by Keyimani L. Alford
First Edition © 2024 by Keyimani L. Alford

Oakland Hills, Milwaukee Rivers:
A Memoir of Survival, Identity, and Purpose
All rights reserved.

No part of this publication may be reproduced, stored in a retrieval system, or transmitted in any form or by any means—electronic, mechanical, photocopying, recording, or otherwise—without prior written permission from the publisher, except by a reviewer who may quote brief passages in a review.

This is the **Second Edition** of *Oakland Hills, Milwaukee Rivers*, revised and expanded with new chapters and a subtitle. This edition replaces the previous edition published under ISBN 979-8-9920869-0-4 & 979-8-9920869-1-1

This is a work of nonfiction. All of the reported incidents occurred as recorded here, to the best of my recollection and records. I have changed the names of all individuals to protect their privacy.

Printed in the United States of America.
Published by Keywords Unlocked, LLC.
6969 N. Port Washington Road, Suite B150, #1025
Glendale, Wisconsin 53217
keywordsunlockedllc@gmail.com
www.drkeyspeaks.com

ISBN: (Paperback) 979-8-9920869-8-0
(eBook) 979-8-9920869-7-3
(Hardcover) 979-8-9920869-9-7

LCCN: 2025911392
Second Edition, First Printing: July 2025
10 9 8 7 6 5 4 3 2

*To every boy, girl, man, and woman who has ever felt
life dealt them an unwinnable hand – I speak to your hope,
your vision, and your future, affirming that you will become everything you were
meant to be.*

"It always seems impossible until it's done."
Nelson Mandela

"Never let someone's opinion become your reality. Never sacrifice who you are because someone else has a problem with it. Love who you are inside and out."
Les Brown

Contents

Author's Note
Why A Second Edition?   iii

Prologue
Between Two Worlds   v

Shaken Foundations   xi

Chapter 01
Lake Merritt   1

Chapter 02
Streetlights   7

Chapter 03
Reckless Adventures   14

Chapter 04
Silent Shadows   23

Chapter 05
Fault Lines   31

Chapter 06
Cover-Ups   38

Restless Soil   43

Chapter 07
Cartoons, Cousins, and Crossroads   45

Chapter 08
Seasons of Change   51

Chapter 09
Between Homes 55

Chapter 10
Survival 60

Chapter 11
A Taste of Freedom 63

Chapter 12
New Home, Old Ways 67

Chapter 13
Rebuilding Roots 74

Chapter 14
Breaking the Cycle 78

Mirrors and Crossroads 87

Chapter 15
The Weight of Regret 89

Chapter 16
Unspoken Expectations 97

Chapter 17
The Voice of Silence 105

Chapter 18
Waiting Patiently 108

Chapter 19
Bridging the Gaps 116

Chapter 20
The Final Goodbye 125

Chapter 21
A Wake-Up Call 132

Chapter 22
Reflections   **139**

Grace & Mercie   144

Chapter 23
The Hidden Cost of Love   **146**

Chapter 24
Divine Covering   **154**

Chapter 25
Lakes, Rivers, and Streams   **162**

Chapter 26
Unconditional Love   **170**

Chapter 27
Highways and Interstates   **181**

Chapter 28
Back Home   **191**

Chapter 29
Family Traditions   **199**

Chapter 30
Transitions   **203**

Chapter 31
The Conclusion   **212**

Epilogue
Unresolved Thoughts   **216**

Acknowledgments   **221**

About the Author   **224**

AUTHOR'S NOTE
Why A Second Edition?

"Never think you can't start over. Every day, the sun rises and sets with a new purpose. To welcome the beginning of a day and say farewell in the same manner."

When I first released *Oakland Hills, Milwaukee Rivers* in 2024, I did so with trembling hands and an open heart. I told myself, *"Just get the story out."* And I did. I bled onto those pages—unfiltered, raw, and honest moments of my life. That version of the book was never about perfection; it was about survival. It was the first time I wholeheartedly owned the truth of what I had lived through.

But something wouldn't let me rest.

As the months passed and readers responded, I began to see what I had left unsaid—not because I was hiding, but because I was still healing and processing what I shared with the world. I had given you snapshots. Glimpses. But not the whole journey. Not the quiet details. Not the moments that shaped me when no one was watching.

So, I went back.

I didn't go back to fix a flaw—I went back to **bring clarity**. The original title reflected my roots, but it didn't clearly show what the book was truly about: survival, identity, and purpose. I owed it to the people who needed this story—especially those who didn't know my name, but would see themselves in these pages—to make it unmistakably clear that this book was for them, too.

This second edition is not just a revised manuscript—it's a deeper invitation. It's the truth I needed time, courage, and grace to write.

I did it to give space for Aunt Grace's impact.

To walk more slowly through the heartbreaks.

To tell the whole story—not just of how I survived, but how I kept going, and the resilience that shaped because of it.

If you read the first edition, thank you for holding space for my voice when it was still trembling. If this is your first encounter with this story, know that every chapter has been reimagined with you in mind.
This is not just a memoir. It's a mirror.

A survival guide.

A reclamation.

A love letter to the kid who made it out—and the man who finally stopped hiding.

Welcome.

Dr. Keyimani L. Alford

PROLOGUE
Between Two Worlds

"We don't get to choose how our story begins or ends. Those belong to different worlds. But what we do in the in-between is what matters most."

Saturday mornings in Oakland felt like borrowed time. I was in my bedroom, sitting on the floor—knees tucked to my chest—watching a 12-inch black-and-white TV that sat on top of an old milk crate. The screen flickered with cartoons, but there was no color, and no sound loud enough to drown out the quiet in the house. My bed sat awkwardly in the middle of the room, its springs seemed to creak even when no one touched them. An old, faded blanket draped across it, wrinkled up like it had stopped caring, too.

There was no dresser. No posters. Just poorly painted walls, a dusty carpeted floor, and the kind of stillness that made time stretch longer than it should.

On weekends, sometimes my stomach would ache from hunger. Not the kind that made you cry—but the kind you got used to. The kind that taught you not to ask questions because you already knew the answer.

OAKLAND HILLS, MILWAUKEE RIVERS

My mom was somewhere in the house, behind a closed door. That's how some days were. Her silence louder than anything on the television. Her absence was louder than her voice and more visible than her presence.

I remember tracing shapes on the floor with my fingers, pretending they were roads out of there, using my imagination to create a world I couldn't touch—but needed to believe in.

Then came the knock.

A slow, steady knock on the front door.

I froze. We didn't get many visitors—not like that. Especially not on a Saturday. I wasn't supposed to open the door, but I didn't need to. A few seconds later, I heard two voices—women—echo through the house like they belonged there. Calm, firm, and familiar.

They talked with my mom for a while, catching up like old friends. Then I heard one of them ask, "Where is he? Where's my nephew?"

My mom answered, "He's back there in his room."

The next knock came softer—closer. My door.

I jumped up from the floor, with my heart pounding.

There she stood. Like a quiet storm.

She didn't ask for permission. She didn't hesitate. And for the first time in a long time, someone was looking *at* me—not past me, not through me, but *at* me. Like I mattered. Like I was worth showing up for.

I didn't know it then, but that knock would change my life.

Oakland taught me how to survive, shrink myself, and pretend everything was fine when everything inside me felt broken. I grew up near the hills, elevated by pride but weighed down by pain, learning to mask my struggle with silence.

But that knock didn't just interrupt the day. It disrupted the direction of my life.

PROLOGUE: BETWEEN TWO WORLDS

It wasn't a rescue wrapped in speeches—it was presence.
Action.
Consistency.
I was brought to Milwaukee—not just to change my zip code, but to rewrite my trajectory.

Where Oakland gave me grit, Milwaukee gave me grace.

Where I learned to be guarded, Milwaukee taught me how to be open.

Where the hills made me climb, the rivers taught me how to flow.

This memoir is about what it means to live—and navigate—between two worlds. Between pain and healing, chaos and calm, abandonment and belonging. It's for every child who's ever sat on the floor of a quiet room, wondering if anyone would come. And for every adult still carrying that child inside who is just wishing to grow up.

Oakland Hills, Milwaukee Rivers is not just a title.

It's a testimony.

A roadmap of struggle and transformation.

* * *

Growing up as an only child came with its own set of assumptions. People often thought my life was stable, privileged, even. They assumed I had everything I needed—that I was spoiled or used to getting my way. While that might be true for some, it couldn't have been further from mine.

My childhood wasn't filled with abundance—it was shaped by lack and survival. Conversations with others often revealed how different my experiences were. But those experiences became the foundation for my resilience.

I used to think survival was the end goal. If I could just make it through—get past the pain, outlast the shame, hide the truth—I'd be okay. But healing doesn't come from what you escape. It comes from what you're willing to face and speak out loud.

OAKLAND HILLS, MILWAUKEE RIVERS

This story—every part of it—was a fight to reclaim myself. Some pages were heavy. Some felt like ripping the bandages off wounds I didn't realize were still bleeding. But every word came from a place of truth I couldn't run from anymore.

You'll walk through my hills—the hard places, the weight I carried, the parts of me that broke and still kept going.
You'll cross my rivers—the changes, the losses, the grace I didn't expect but desperately needed.

And maybe, somewhere in the tension between the two, you'll see a piece of yourself too.

This isn't the full story. But it's the part I'm ready to share. The rest—what's still being wrestled with—will come in time.

But for now, I've opened the door.

Come in. The story begins here.

SHAKEN FOUNDATIONS

"Some things break to reveal what was never truly steady to begin with."

They say the ground doesn't have to crack for your world to fall apart. Sometimes, it's the silence in the hallway, the hunger that teaches you how to numb, and the knock on the door that changes everything.

This part of the story marks the beginning of turmoil. Childhood in Oakland offered little room for stillness—not the comforting kind. Instead, it presented lessons hidden within earthquakes, both literal and emotional. These chapters brim with aftershocks: unmet needs, unspoken fears, and sudden goodbyes.

Here is where we learn to walk carefully—how to read the room, brace for the next hit, and keep smiling even when your hands are shaking inside. These are the stories of first friends, fractured trust, and a boy figuring out how to protect the parts of himself that the world had no interest in saving.

This is where survival became a language I learned without realizing I was fluent.

CHAPTER 01
Lake Merritt

"Friendships are like mirrors, reflecting what stands before them. Choose yours wisely, as friendships, like flowers, fade if not watered."

Looking back, I sometimes wonder how I ended up in some of the wild situations I did. Even as a little kid, I embarked on adventures that, in hindsight, probably weren't the safest or wisest ways to spend a childhood afternoon. Perhaps being an only child gave me the independence to make those questionable decisions, or maybe it was fate's way of preparing me for the challenges life would throw my way later. Either way, growing up on East 24th Street in Oakland had a way of turning even the most mundane days into unforgettable memories.

Our neighborhood was a lively place, brimming with character and excitement, nestled in the heart of California's abundant citrus groves. It was nearly impossible to walk down a street without passing trees heavy with lemons, oranges, or grapefruits. Our apartment was at the base of a hill in a duplex, with my family occupying the lower level and our neighbors—a Native American family—living above us. Their son, London, was about my age, and we hit it off almost instantly. His family, with younger parents and playful energy, was full of laughter and joy. His dad and uncle, with their sun-kissed skin and long, straight black hair, exuded warmth and vibrancy, transforming our shared porch into a welcoming hub for anyone and everyone.

London and I were inseparable, roaming the neighborhood as if it were our kingdom. Across the street, thick vines twisted up walls and fences, where we played, making it perfect for climbing. They stood between the neighborhood church, where we'd get our weekly fix of powdered milk, government cheese, and all the other essentials to supplement our meals. A few houses down lived Diego, one of our regular friends. He owned a Sega Genesis—the holy grail of gaming systems in our eyes. We spent hours in his living room, transfixed by Sonic the Hedgehog, our fingers flying over the controllers as we tried to beat level after level. Diego's backyard was like a hidden oasis. Among its treasures was a kumquat tree, laden with small, vibrant orange fruits that became my favorite snack. I still remember the taste—juicy, with just the right blend of sweet and tart, about the size of a ping-pong ball, with a brown seed in the center. We'd climb onto the roof of his garage to reach the ripest kumquats, savoring each bite as we tossed the seeds to the ground below. There was also a grapefruit tree in his yard, but those fruits were bitter unless we covered them in sugar—a rarity unless we were craving a change from our usual kumquat harvest.

The block was also home to a few citrus trees we'd raid occasionally, picking huge, juicy oranges and tart lemons straight from the branches. Biting into an orange fresh off the tree, its sweetness flooding our mouths, felt like tasting a slice of California sunshine itself. We'd often launch the peels at each other, laughing as we dodged the flying bits of fruit skin.

London's family was close-knit, always gathering on the porch to catch up on each other's lives. My mom and I felt comfortable with them, a trust built over countless small interactions and the occasional borrowing of sugar or cooking oil. It was the kind of neighborly bond that felt like family, and that sense of belonging also extended to the kids. London and I spent hours on our bikes, speeding down the streets of Oakland and exploring the corners of our neighborhood with boundless energy. Diamond Park was one of our favorite destinations. It had a small creek that wound along a narrow path, ending in a gentle waterfall next to a golf course. We'd wade into the water,

LAKE MERRITT

fishing out golf balls to bring home—our little treasure hunt. But the real fun began when we got them back home. Tucked between the houses, crouched like conspirators, we waited for cars to drive down the street. As headlights drew close, one of us would throw a ball into the road, where it would hit the pavement with a loud crack, bouncing wildly in the direction of the oncoming car. Sometimes, we'd hold our breath as a ball would smack against the car's bumper—a tiny, harmless rebellion against the world of adults. In that moment, we felt invincible.

And yet, fear was our constant shadow. We'd barely wait to see the driver's reaction before darting off in all directions, legs pumping, laughter mingling with the thrill of knowing we'd gotten away—just this once. But beneath the thrill lurked the understanding that, if ever caught, our parents would have more than a few stern words waiting for us. We knew we were tempting fate each time, yet the thrill of defiance was irresistible. The thrill of a risk taken, a secret kept, a rule broken—just one more time. Another piece of our childhood adventures.

* * *

One summer day, London's family invited me to join them on a trip to Lake Merritt. The lake wasn't just water—it was Oakland's heartbeat. A space where joggers, families, and dreamers gathered to lose track of time. When I asked my mom if I could go, she didn't hesitate. She trusted London's family, and I trusted the idea that something about this day would matter.

I wore my favorite white T-shirt with blue trim and a rainbow design, and my worn jean shorts that had seen better days. The sun had full authority that day, resting on our shoulders with warmth that felt personal. The water shimmered like it was stitched with gold, its ripples catching the light just right. The path around the lake—just over three miles—was alive: joggers pounding pavement, kids weaving between walkers on bikes, and couples locked in soft conversation.

Palm trees, a staple in the California landscape, stood tall like silent elders, watching as we moved. Ducks glided across the water, paddleboats drifted lazily, and the scent of blooming flowers and grilled food danced in the breeze. Everything felt wide open, effortless, and free.

OAKLAND HILLS, MILWAUKEE RIVERS

Alford, K. (2024) *Lake Merritt* [Photograph]. Oakland, California: Keywords Unlocked, LLC

But freedom—real or imagined—can blur judgment.

Later that afternoon, London's dad and uncle stopped at a liquor store. They came out smiling, holding a massive, round glass jug of wine that looked like it belonged in a cartoon. It had a handle on the side. They were in a good mood holding it, maybe based on the anticipation of what its contents would bring or conversations they had in the store itself.

Then they offered us a sip.

To us, it felt like a joke. A dare, even. Like puffing my mom's cigarette butts from the ashtray and convincing myself it didn't count. I took a gulp. Then another. The warm burn in my throat made me feel grown. And I felt like nothing could touch me.

But freedom doesn't always feel like a warning. Sometimes it feels like laughter on your lips and heat on your skin—right before the shame shows up.

We walked through the neighborhood, and somewhere along the way, I stripped off my shirt, drunk off that jug of rebellion, and left it on someone's porch like it didn't matter. Like, I didn't care who saw me.

LAKE MERRITT

* * *

When we finally reached home, my mom took one look at me and knew. Her gaze was a mixture of surprise and something else, a little amused but mostly unimpressed. She exchanged words with London's dad and uncle that I couldn't quite catch, and I remember her gentle hand guiding me into the house. She didn't scold or punish me; she just ushered me to the bathroom, ran a lukewarm bath, and watched as I splashed around, sobering up. That night, I fell asleep fast, drifting off with the memories of our adventure still playing behind my eyelids.

I woke up the next morning, the remnants of my first brush with rebellion fading, but the memories firmly in place. It had been a wild day, one I'll never forget—a glimpse into the unpredictable world of grown-ups and a rite of passage that, looking back, was both absurd and memorable. The summer continued, and although my mom didn't let me hang out with London's family as much afterward, those memories stayed with me. They were just one of many that made up the beautiful, chaotic tapestry of my Oakland childhood, when the world felt a little bigger, a little brighter, and every day was a new adventure.

Reflecting on those summer days, those kumquat-stained fingers, and those mischievous grins weren't just random snapshots of childhood—they were the blueprints of something deeper taking root. We weren't just kids playing in the streets or throwing golf balls at bumpers for laughs. Without knowing it, we were learning how to navigate risk, trust instinct, and protect the ones we called family. Even then, my loyalty ran deep. If you were with me— really with me—I'd stand beside you, no matter how reckless the road ahead. It didn't matter if we were climbing fences we weren't supposed to, daring each other to touch the electric thrill of the unknown, or sipping from bottles we didn't fully understand. If you were my friend, I was riding with you.

That same loyalty later complicated my life. I held on to people who had already let go, thinking shared history should be enough. I thought leaving meant giving up on everything we'd had. But that's the thing about early lessons—they don't always come with instruction manuals. They're lived, felt, and sometimes misinterpreted. Still, they stay with you.

OAKLAND HILLS, MILWAUKEE RIVERS

The curiosity that once had me peeling back citrus bark and exploring creeks behind playgrounds became the same curiosity that pushed me to search for more in life. More than what the neighborhood had to offer. More than what my zip code suggested I was worth. I was always asking questions, wondering what was around the next block, behind the next door, beyond the boundaries someone else had set for me. That restless wonder became my engine—sometimes leading me to trouble, yes—but just as often pulling me toward purpose. Toward something better.

And resilience was born right there on East 24th Street. In the late-night bike rides. In the long baths after bad decisions. And, in the sound of my mom's voice calling me home before the streetlights got too bright. I didn't know it then, but I was learning how to bounce back. How to laugh after getting caught. How to forgive myself and try again. Who would've known my carefree days of childhood would become rehearsals for a life that would ask me to be strong, loyal, and brave… again and again.

Lake Merritt wasn't just a place. It was a preview. A mirror. A reminder that the boy who ran through those Oakland streets didn't disappear. He would one day grow up to revisit everything he learned—every wild decision, every scraped knee, every hidden tear to become the foundation I'd build my future on.

CHAPTER 02
Streetlights

"Protection is often wrapped in love. Those who care deeply want to ensure you're here to experience another day. Cherish their concern and hold it as a precious gift in your life."

The streets of Oakland had a way of leaving their mark, etching themselves into me even as life shifted and addresses changed. Though we moved just a few blocks away, the rhythm of the city—its gritty essence and unspoken rules—remained as familiar as my own reflection. Every corner, every cracked sidewalk still felt like home, holding stories I wasn't ready to let go of, even as the scenery shifted slightly around me. By then, I had grown older but still carried the same build—a tall, scrawny, dark-skinned Black boy. My hair was thick and rough, and it regularly did its own thing. Kinda like the neighborhood. Back then, haircuts weren't regular. When I got one, it was from friends still learning the craft. The cuts were uneven, but it didn't matter. I was just a kid, and the world had more pressing matters than how neatly my hair was cut.

Each morning, I'd wake early, the weight of sleep still lingering, and carefully make my bed. Always neat and precise, it was my small act of creating order in a world that often felt unpredictable. As a kid, I never thought too much about the future. It was too far ahead, a hazy thing I couldn't grasp. But one thing was clear: I wanted to be a doctor. The thought of healing people became a passion in those quiet moments. Each glance at my face carried an unspoken yearning, a desire to understand and mend, not just the wounds I could see, but the ones hidden beneath. Those moments stirred something profound within me—a calling I couldn't quite articulate, but I felt it like a soft whisper, urging me to step into a world where I could help others—a place of healing, support, and impact. Maybe my chronic asthma made me so acutely aware of the fragility of life. At times, I'd sit on the floor by my bedroom window, gasping for breath after an attack, watching the world go by, wondering how it would feel to take a deep, uninterrupted breath. The sensation of air filling my lungs was something I cherished deeply, like a gift, and I wanted to help others feel that way too. Regardless, in those fleeting moments of solitude, I knew my life had a purpose. I had to figure out exactly what that purpose was—my contribution to a world with so many challenges.

Life wasn't easy, but it was manageable. I had a few things on my side—good friends, my mom, and the freedom of youth. The neighborhood felt like an extension of our homes. It was where we lived, played, and grew together. My friends and I raced our bikes down the city's narrow streets, speeding down hills, indifferent to the cracks in the sidewalk or the cars that sped by. We had no reason to be afraid, no responsibilities weighing us down. The weather always made us feel like we could do anything—like we owned the streets. Some days, we raced through the neighborhood, shouting and laughing as we swerved on the sidewalks, pretending we owned it and that the whole world was ours to conquer.

But there were other days when we didn't need bikes to entertain us. We found something else on those days: something a little more absurd, but infinitely more fun. We turned my friend Walter's front yard into our wrestling ring. Walter was the only one in the neighborhood who had real grass. The rest of us had dirt yards or cracked concrete, but Walter's house sat halfway up the hill, surrounded by a mountain of green, though sometimes brown grass, as only California could know. His family had a pretty nice house that made you feel like there was something a little different about them—something that felt out of reach for us, but in a good way. His parents were kind, so naturally, it became the perfect spot for our weekly wrestling matches.

Alford, K. (2024) *Neighborhood* [Photograph]. Oakland, California: Keywords Unlocked, LLC

The neighborhood was hilly, featuring steep inclines and declines, creating a landscape that became our personal playground. My house sat at the bottom of the hill, directly across from the hospital, while Walter's house was a small trek up, nestled halfway along the slope. At the base of his house lay ten steps leading up to his porch—a small climb, but enough to make us feel like we had reached something important. As kids, we would gather there, with the porch serving as our "top rope," the perfect place to leap from, pretending we were the characters we admired on TV.

I was obsessed with Hulk Hogan. We all had our favorites, and we'd wrestle in the yard, leaping from the porch like it was Madison Square Garden.. We were either Andre the Giant, Macho Man Randy Savage, or the Ultimate

Warrior. There we were, a group of kids who had never been to a wrestling match but were convinced we were just as capable of pulling off a suplex as the pros on TV. We tumbled through the grass, each of us taking turns pretending to be the hero, the villain, or the referee, infusing every match with colorful commentary to declare the winner. As the referee, one of us would dramatically slide across the grass, pounding the ground with a hand while shouting, "One... two... three!" It felt as if an imaginary bell chimed in the background, solidifying the victory and crowning the champion of the match. Those were the days when we didn't worry about anything—about grades, the future, or the world beyond our small corner of Oakland. We didn't think about our families' struggles or the difficulties we might one day face. We were free, playing in a yard that was the definition of simplicity, yet it was the center of the universe for us. No worries, no responsibilities—just the pure bliss of being kids. The laughter rang out like music in the air, mixing with the scent of fresh grass and the sound of our footsteps running up and down the hill.

Those were the moments that would stay with me forever—moments when I truly felt like I could conquer the world, when life was simpler than it would ever be again. But like all good things, those days came to an end. The seasons changed, and so did we. However, the memories, the simple joys of being a kid in the neighborhood, never faded. Even now, when I think of my childhood, I recall those weekends in Walter's front yard, the feeling of weightlessness as we threw ourselves into the air, not a care in the world, not a worry on our minds.

After school on weekdays, the neighborhood transformed into our kingdom once the homework was finished and the books were tucked away. The sun sank lower in the sky, casting a warm golden glow across the street, and we raced out of our houses to gather. My friends and I didn't have much, but we had the freedom of youth, and that was enough to fill our hearts with joy. We were unstoppable.

But as the day wound down and the shadows grew longer, something else shifted in the air. The streetlights flickered on, one by one, their pale yellow glow cutting through the darkening sky, and we felt a subtle pressure like an invisible hand pulling us toward home. It was time for us to return, to call it a night before the world outside began to feel less safe, less forgiving.

The first sign of this change was always the unmistakable sound of my mother's voice. Most kids heard their names and ran the other way—either trying to squeeze out five more minutes of freedom or avoid whatever chore waited behind that call. But there was something different about how my mother's voice pierced the air. It wasn't just sound; it was spirit. It carried weight and warmth, sharpness and softness—a language that only those raised by Black mothers could fully understand.

That voice was correction wrapped in concern. It was discipline laced with devotion. And it didn't always feel good—not to a child who just wanted to play until the sky went black and the stars blinked awake. Back then, I didn't always recognize her voice as grace. I mistook it for nagging, interruption, or a sound that ruined my fun. But it was none of those things. It was her way of covering me, of keeping her only child whole in a world that wasn't always kind to boys who looked like me.

My mom had no partner standing beside her. No one to help carry the weight of protecting me from the dangers I couldn't see and the ones I didn't yet believe were real. So, she compensated the only way she knew how—with presence. With a voice that reached corners of the block faster than a phone call. With a tone that didn't ask for permission—it demanded attention. She didn't hover out of paranoia; she stood guard out of necessity. Her love was a lighthouse. Unyielding. Unapologetic. But I was too young, too naïve to know that her warning voice was a form of mercy—that her instructions were her way of saying, "Live long enough to make your own choices."

As a kid, I sometimes felt embarrassed, even irritated, by the intensity of her love. I didn't understand the fear tucked behind her voice, the sleepless nights wrapped around her prayers, or the silence she sat in after the door closed behind me. She had witnessed what the world could do to Black boys, especially those without backup. Thus, her voice became both shield and sword. She used it to bring me back before the darkness could snatch me. And even when I didn't express it or stormed inside with an attitude, something deep within me trusted that voice.

Now I know love doesn't always come dressed in hugs and soft words. Most days, it was in her calling my name. She'd stand by the living room window of our two-story duplex, which faced west, perfectly aligned with the street where we played. The window would creak open with a familiar sound, and I knew I was about to hear her voice call my name even before the words came. It was never just "Keyimani" when I was a child. No, she'd shorten it to something more intimate, familiar, a name that felt like a song—a melody only she could sing. "Key Key," she'd call, her voice rising in pitch as the second word seemed to stretch out like it had its own life. There was something powerful about the way she said it. The "e" in "Key Key" would stretch longer than the rest, as if her love and concern poured out with each syllable.

If I didn't respond right away, another "Key Key" would ring through the air, this time her voice louder and carrying up the hill, echoing through the neighborhood like the sound of a bell tolling. It was a call that should not be ignored, not even by the most lost in thought or the busiest among us. Her voice pulled me in with a strength that made the whole block pause—even if we were mid-conversation or mid-laugh, we all heard it. We all knew the sound of her voice. Even my friends scattered around the block would stop what they were doing, turn to me, and shout in unison, "Keyimani, your mom is calling you!" And I would feel that mix of love and dread settle into my chest. There was no way to escape it.

No matter how badly I wanted to stay out a little longer, I knew it was time to go. I had to obey because her voice wore the robe of rules, curfews, and tough conversations you don't want to hear. I had to respond, so I would yell back, "I'm coming!" as I heard her call. I would start my descent down the hill with all the speed my legs could manage, the words tumbling out of me like a promise, an assurance that I would make it back before I got into trouble. And believe me, you did not want to be late. It wasn't just about getting to bed on time—it was about respect. Respect for my mom, respect for the rules that had been set in place to protect me, and respect for the boundaries that shaped my world. Growing up in a Black family meant having a deep understanding of this respect. There was an unspoken rule in our neighborhood: "I better not catch you with the streetlights on." This was more than just a curfew. It was a protective shield, a way for our parents to keep us safe, even when they weren't watching us every second.

The streetlights, those humble, glowing sentinels of the evening, served as our alarm clock. When the lights flickered on, it was time to head home, no matter what we were doing or where we were in our games. We knew that when the streetlights came on, we had already pushed our luck long enough.

And so, each day, as the streetlights illuminated the corners of the neighborhood, we felt that pull—the call to come inside and return to the safety of our homes. In those moments, we didn't just feel like children being sent in for the night. We felt the weight of something much bigger than us: the love and protection of our parents, who looked out for us even when we didn't fully understand the reasons behind their rules.

CHAPTER 03
Reckless Adventures

"Freedom is given, but can be lost with one bad decision. Choose what your future looks like because chances don't come often."

Oakland, California, was something serious, a place that shaped me in ways I didn't fully understand until I grew older. The days spent riding bikes through the neighborhood felt like they lasted forever, filled with the carefree joy that only childhood could bring. My friends and I would pedal up and down the steep hills, our tires crunching against the asphalt as we made our way to the corner store, where everything stopped for a while. There, we'd pool together what little money we had and buy our favorite candies—Now and Laters, a treat that was as cheap as it was satisfying. Just ten cents a pack, they came in a wild array of flavors— from sour apple to my favorite: passion fruit. The tangy sweetness would explode in your mouth, lingering long after the candy was gone. The chocolate flavor, though... that wasn't my thing. It was too heavy, too bitter for my taste, but I'd buy it sometimes to have something to offer if someone else didn't have enough change.

The neighborhood was an odd mix of beauty and danger, a landscape that defied convention. In Oakland, the geography was quirky—hills and valleys carved through the city like natural pathways, with some parts flat and others rising sharply. As I reflect on it now, my house was situated in a sort of valley, tucked away at the bottom of the hill. From our window, you could see the busy street ahead, cars speeding by; for us, that street was both an obstacle and a bridge. We crossed it daily, dodging traffic and feeling the adrenaline spike in our chests. Back then, it wasn't as scary, though. People were kinder, perhaps more patient with the children who raced across the pavement on bikes, their legs pumping with determination. Drivers would stop for us—an unspoken understanding passed between pedestrians and drivers: kids, let them go. You didn't have to be in a rush all the time. It was a different world.

And when we weren't darting across that busy street, we cruised to Lake Merritt. The lake was a hidden gem in the city's heart, a place I couldn't help but feel drawn to. Maybe it was the serenity of the water that always seemed to calm my mind, or perhaps the occasional crawfish scuttled across the rocks, their tiny claws clicking in the quiet afternoon. I'd crouch low to study them, fascinated by their small, armored bodies. And then there were the ducks. They'd waddle around, seemingly unbothered by our presence, quacking lazily as if they owned the place. That's the thing about Lake Merritt—it wore peace like a mask, but tension always lurked beneath. In the backdrop, the hills rose sharply, steep and almost menacing, with houses perched precariously on the slopes. It made me think of earthquakes and how they could hit at any moment, reminding me that nature here was as beautiful as it was unpredictable. But, like the ducks, I didn't worry. We lived with the uncertainty and made the best of it.

Saturdays were the best days, blending into one long, uninterrupted adventure. We'd spend our mornings enjoying cartoons—the classics. He-Man, the mighty warrior wielding his sword, and Transformers, where robots transformed into cars and planes. Scooby-Doo was always a favorite; the gang's antics made us laugh. Voltron, a tale of five lion robots combining into one massive defender of the galaxy, left us feeling like we too could be superheroes. Afterward, our ritual was simple: finish our weekend chores and meet up.

Our chores were never easy. No one escaped them. There were no exemptions for the kids, especially regarding cleaning. We'd gripe and groan about the work that needed to be done—scrubbing the bathroom tiles, washing the walls, folding laundry, and cleaning the dishes. But the worst, by far, was cleaning out the refrigerator. The smell of stale leftovers and the remnants of meals gone by always felt like the fridge was somehow a reflection of how messy our lives could get. The drawers had to come out, each scrubbed clean and wiped down until they gleamed. It felt like an eternity; no matter how often I did it, I could never get used to it.

Our home was small, a two-bedroom apartment nestled in the heart of the neighborhood. It had that cozy, cramped feeling—like everything was within arm's reach. You'd walk up a flight of stairs and suddenly find yourself in the middle of the apartment. The living room was at the front, and beyond that was the kitchen, the heart of our home. It was small too; nothing fancy, but it had everything we needed. The walls creaked under the weight of memories, and the floors were worn from years of use, but it was ours. My mom had these long plastic beads hanging in the kitchen doorway, and every time you walked through them, they made a noise—clattering and clinking. I always thought they were like an alarm, a way for her to know when I was sneaking into the kitchen. I'd creep in late at night, hungry from all the running around, looking for anything to snack on. But it never failed—just as I was about to open the fridge, I'd hear her voice from the other room, "Key Key, get out that kitchen! You aren't hungry!" she'd say, a sharp, loving tone in her voice that let me know my time was up. The fridge door would snap shut, and I'd sigh, disappointed knowing she was right. Maybe I wasn't hungry after all.

The kitchen was a small yet familiar world that always seemed to carry the hum of activity, whether it was my mom preparing dinner or me sneaking in for a midnight snack. It wasn't much, but it was home, with its short walls and old cabinets slightly chipped around the edges. The tile countertop featured a design reminiscent of something from a Latin American country. Its pattern of muted colors and geometric shapes made the space feel quaint, as if it were stuck in time, possessing stories to tell if you just listened closely enough.

The sink sat in the center of the kitchen, its small window offering a view of the neighbor's house across the way. That window became my little window to the world outside, providing a glimpse into someone else's life while I stood there washing dishes or filling a glass of water. The view wasn't much—just the brick exterior of the neighbor's house—but sometimes I'd stare at the weathered window frame, watching the dust collect on the sill, my mind wandering as I imagined all sorts of stories about the people who lived there.

Next to the sink was another cabinet—our makeshift pantry. The shelves were lined with cans of beans, boxes of powdered milk from the church pantry, and bags of rice, each item a small staple of our daily life. The refrigerator sat near the stove at the south end of the wall. It was an odd layout; the fridge and stove faced each other across the narrow space, and you couldn't open both simultaneously without feeling like a contortionist. It wasn't ideal, but we made it work. And for all the awkwardness, it was functional. Despite its tight quarters, the kitchen held an energy all its own—one of simple sustenance and quiet moments shared between mother and son.

Beyond the refrigerator, another small entrance led to the hallway that connected the kitchen to the rest of the house. My mom's bedroom was on the other side of the kitchen wall, which felt like a sanctuary to me. Her bed—well, it was something special. It wasn't just any bed; it was a king-sized waterbed, and as a kid, it felt like a whole new world when I'd plop down into it. The water would ripple beneath me, sending waves across the surface, and I'd ride them with the kind of carefree joy only a child can experience. But, of course, I couldn't stay there for long. I knew better than to mess up her pillows or make too much noise. She'd be home soon and know exactly where I'd been. However, the memory of those moments—floating on the waves of the waterbed—would stay with me, an indulgent secret of my childhood.

Just next door was my bedroom. It was small but mine, tucked away behind a thin wall separating it from my mom's room. The room was just big enough to fit my twin-sized bed, which was narrow yet comfortable enough for a boy who spent more time running around the neighborhood than sleeping. A small dresser sat beside the bed, holding my clothes, and in the corner of the room stood my 14-inch black-and-white television. It wasn't much by today's standards, but it was a world of adventure to me. My favorite shows flickered across the screen, the characters' voices crackling out of the small speaker while I lay in bed, dreaming of being a hero or an explorer in far-off lands. The living room, with its full-color TV, was where my mom usually sat, but my room was a place where I could retreat—a quiet sanctuary where I could imagine all the things I might one day become.

The bathroom was just as small down the hallway, but it served its purpose. The tub, the sink, and the window that overlooked the garages and two apartments perched in the middle of the hill—the view was nothing spectacular, but it was enough. From the bathroom window, I could see the rooftops of some houses in the neighborhood, their angles and shapes a puzzle of architecture that looked out of place amid the hills. The garages, with their fading paint and cluttered spaces, were part of the landscape I had grown accustomed to. I would look out that window sometimes while brushing my teeth or washing my face, wondering about the people who lived in those apartments, their lives, and how their stories differed from mine.

* * *

It was a Saturday, one of those lazy afternoons that stretched endlessly before us, with no schoolwork to tie us down and no chores to distract us. As restless as ever, my friends and I decided it was time for something different. Riding bikes up and down the same streets and circling the same parks wasn't cutting it anymore. We were craving a new adventure, something bold and offbeat. We wanted to stir things up. So, without much thought or any plan, we made the collective decision: we'd go into the hospital.

Highland Hospital loomed over us, just across the street from where we lived. It wasn't a place we visited for fun, of course, but to us, it was close enough to feel like part of our neighborhood yet distant enough to seem like an adventure. The idea of sneaking through its sterile halls, perhaps taking the elevators to random floors, running down long corridors, and causing mischief felt thrilling. We weren't the brightest then, and there was no deep rationale behind it. We weren't contemplating the consequences or the seriousness of our actions. We just wanted to break free from the dull routine of our usual Saturdays and do something different, something our bikes couldn't offer.

Alford, K. (2024) *Highland Hospital* [Photograph]. Oakland, California: Keywords Unlocked, LLC

We entered through one of the less glamorous side doors of the hospital. The halls were too quiet for our liking, but that only added to the excitement. The long, polished floors gleamed under the sterile fluorescent lights. The air smelled faintly of antiseptic, a sharp, clean scent that made the place feel like something out of a movie. The silence was broken by the sound of our sneakers tapping against the tiles; the soft thud of our footsteps rang louder than usual in the stillness. We took the elevator up to the second floor, then the third, running down the hallways and popping in and out of rooms where no one was. We were living in the moment, feeling like rebels, with adrenaline buzzing through our veins as we disrupted the hospital's normally calm, orderly rhythm.

That is until we heard the voice. It came from nowhere, deep and commanding, cutting through the quiet like a blade. "Hey kids, who are you with?" It was a voice that stopped us dead in our tracks, the kind of voice that made every muscle in our bodies freeze. My heart dropped into my stomach. We all turned, frozen in place, staring wide-eyed at the hospital security guard who had emerged from a hallway like a figure in a nightmare. We didn't have an answer. All we could think to do was run, instinct taking over. Our legs moved before we realized what we were doing, and we bolted down the hallway, rounding corners, hoping somehow to escape, hoping we'd slip through the cracks and make it back outside. But it didn't take long for reality to catch up with us.

We were fast, but not fast enough. The security guard was quick, and within moments, we were caught. Our hearts pounded in our chests as he escorted us down to a lower floor, a cold, sterile place where a set of heavy metal doors closed behind us with a sickening finality. We were in a holding cell—yes, a holding cell—the kind they use for people who are in trouble. It was a place I'd only heard about in stories or seen in the movies, but now I was in one. It was where you don't know whether to sit or stand, where the silence feels suffocating, and every second feels like an eternity. I was terrified. I tried not to show it, but inside, I was panicking. The thought of what my mom would do if she found out crept into my mind like a shadow. If she ever knew that the security guards of a hospital had caught me, she would kill me. I could already hear the sharp crack of the braided switch in her hand, the one she'd make me pick from the yard. She'd have that look where her anger was so palpable you could feel it in the air. And worse, I'd already be crying before returning to the house.

The thought was worse than anything else, and my mind started to spiral. What if they called the police? What if they told our parents? What if this was it? What would happen to us then? Would I be sent to jail?

The hours seemed to stretch endlessly, even though I knew it couldn't have been more than an hour. Each minute ticked by slowly, painfully, as we sat there, all of us silently imagining the worst. We were in so much trouble, and the weight of that realization felt suffocating. We weren't bad kids, not really. But we had crossed a line, doing something reckless without considering the consequences, and now we were paying the price. But then, something strange happened. Just when I thought we were doomed, when I thought the police were going to show up or our parents were going to burst through those doors, the guards came back. They didn't call the police. They didn't call our parents. They just let us go. I remember the moment clearly. They told us, in no uncertain terms, that we were never to return to the hospital again. It wasn't a threat, more like a final warning, and for some reason, that was enough. We didn't argue. We didn't try to explain ourselves. We just nodded, too shaken to do anything else, and left.

We were free. We'd been let off with a warning, but the experience had left its mark. The shock of being locked in that cell, of feeling helpless and trapped, was enough to ensure I never wanted to experience anything like it again. It served as a brutal, unsettling reminder of how quickly things could go wrong, how close we'd come to making our worst fears a reality. It was more than just a "lesson"—it was a kind of trauma that sticks with you long after the incident is over.

To this day, my mom never knew what happened. I never told her. And I never will. I can't bring myself to share something about that day—about the fear, the shame, and the relief of being let go. It was a moment that marked me, but I also knew I could never tell her. Some things are better left unsaid, buried in the past, which was one of those things. We'd gotten away with it. But I knew that, somehow, the cost of that freedom was something I would carry with me forever.

That day might have ended with a warning, but the emotional weight stayed with me far longer. We had been let go—but only just. While it felt like freedom at the moment, the truth is, it was a dangerous kind of freedom. The kind that leaves too much room for mistakes. The kind that, without guidance, can get you caught up in cycles you can't pray your way out of.

Growing up in Oakland, we didn't always understand the difference between free and lost. We thought freedom meant being out late without anyone checking on us. We believed it was doing what we wanted without considering the consequences. However, real freedom—lasting freedom—requires structure. It needs direction. Otherwise, it transforms into a trap with invisible bars. One wrong move, one moment of being in the wrong place at the wrong time, and suddenly that freedom becomes a courtroom, a cell, or worse.

In places like Oakland, Black boys walk a tightrope every single day, and the margin for error is razor thin. The system doesn't extend grace to kids who look like us. We aren't seen as children who made bad choices; we're labeled as threats, statistics, or lost causes. What's terrifying is how quickly you can go from laughing with your friends to being locked behind a steel door. All it takes is one reckless decision, one act without a second thought, and your whole life can shift.

We weren't bad kids. But we were vulnerable—unguarded, unchecked, and sometimes too bold for our own good. The truth is, without the kind of intentional guidance that shows you who you are and what you're worth, the streets will assign you an identity of their own. And Oakland, for all its beauty, didn't play fair. It was a place where being a Black boy meant you had to grow up fast or risk not growing up at all. Where freedom could fool you into thinking you were safe when, in reality, you were standing at the edge of something dangerous.

I reflect on that day and realize how easily things could've gone another way. We could've been booked. We could've had records that followed us before we even had a chance to know who we were. And no one would've asked what we were going through, or why we did what we did. That's the part that still hits me. How close we came. How fragile it all was.

So now, when I think about freedom, I consider it differently. I see it as something earned through wisdom, knowing your worth, and understanding that sometimes the most powerful move isn't doing what you want— but knowing when to stop. To protect you, your future, and the consequences of making a wrong decision.

CHAPTER 04
Silent Shadows

"How we decide to move forward depends on our desire to stay bound or be liberated."

Twice it happened—moments of violation I experienced as a child that I kept to myself. Reflecting on those times, I wonder why I never told anyone until now. Perhaps I didn't think anything was wrong, or maybe I believed no one would believe me, but it happened.

Growing up as an only child, the absence of siblings drove me to form my own family with friends and relatives, seeking out those small, meaningful connections that added texture and color to my world. My days revolved around neighborhood friendships and family visits, as I navigated the streets of East Oakland like any other kid on the block. Without brothers or sisters to share in my childhood adventures, I roamed freely and built bonds wherever I could, finding family in familiar faces and friendships in familiar places.

One family I often visited lived just a short walk away. The neighborhood was full of movement and memories; we moved a few times when I was young, but somehow, my mom kept us close to our roots. I think she liked the familiarity of East Oakland, the faces of neighbors we knew, and the comfort of Bella Vista Elementary, where I'd made my first set of close friends. She wanted me to have that sense of stability, of belonging. And maybe, too, she wanted the safety net that came with being known—being Maddy's son gave me street-wide protection; I could walk the few blocks to my friends' houses or the corner store without worry.

That corner store, small and sweet-smelling like a jar of candy, was where I spent much of my time. My mom had a tab with the store's owner, a simple arrangement that made it easy to pick up essentials or, if I was lucky, a few sweets. It was a familiar stop on my small route of freedom. Back then, we were on welfare, and our checks arrived like clockwork every first and fifteenth of the month. I still remember those food stamps—brightly colored, crinkly paper bills you'd tear out from booklets. To a kid, they were golden tickets for small pleasures like candy or chips.

* * *

One visit stands out in my memory. I was headed to see Jessie, a cousin of mine who lived just a few blocks from us, over a hill that gently sloped into the street. Their apartment sat above a Chinese restaurant, the scent of fried rice and chow mein wafting up from below. Simply reaching the building felt like a journey, the hill providing a slightly different view of the neighborhood with each step up or down.

This time, I asked my mom if I could stay the night. Spending the night was a rare treat, an opportunity to escape into someone else's world. With Erma's permission, Jessie's mother, and additional confirmation from a nod by Sherman, my uncle and Jessie's father, I settled in for the night, excited to have another boy around to play with. Jessie shared a room with his sister, Tanya, and although space was tight, he seemed to relish the chance to have a friend all to himself for the evening.

We spent our time talking, laughing, playing, and inventing games, filling the hours with the excitement that only two boys on a sleepover could know. His room was cramped yet inviting, with toys scattered here and there, a warm chaos that felt like a brother's presence. They even had a closet big enough to hide in, an accidental hideaway where we'd stuff ourselves, whispering secrets and giggling as we muffled our voices to avoid detection by wandering adults. It felt like our own private world, a tiny space away from the rest of life, where it was just us and whatever stories we wanted to tell.

Yet looking back now, through the lens of time and experience, I realize that some things were... different. It wasn't just the cramped quarters or the hushed tones we spoke in, but rather a small discomfort that was easy to overlook at the moment. Sometimes, in our cramped closet hideout, I felt the boundary of play disappear into something else. A whisper here, a strange touch there, all dismissed as the quirks of family dynamics at the time. I brushed off anything that made me feel uneasy, thinking perhaps it was part of the odd way families sometimes interacted.

It's strange how a child's mind creates reasons to explain the unexplained, finding ways to rationalize things that feel wrong but seem beyond question. I didn't understand then, but those moments shaped me in subtle ways I can see now. They were the beginnings of an awareness, a quiet realization that sometimes, even among family, things could slip from innocent to strange, from playful to painful. It stemmed more from a misguided curiosity about touching rather than any genuine understanding of intimacy. Even so, I now recognize it for what it truly was: a form of sexual violation.

It happened a few times, and at that age, I had no concept that it could be labeled as a "gay" activity. My mom had a friend who often hung out at our house, and although I now understand she was transgender, it all felt completely normal to me at the time. Yet, I never spoke about it to anyone.

* * *

Then it happened again: that feeling of quiet confusion mixed with fear—the kind that sits at the back of your mind but never quite makes itself clear. I remember that night vividly, as though every detail was etched into my memory with unusual clarity. It was the kind of night that seemed perfectly still, where even the usual sounds—the creak of the old house settling, the occasional car rumbling by outside—seemed to hush themselves, leaving only silence.

My mom, ever compassionate, had invited her friend Lisa and her two sons, Jacob and Jeremiah, to stay with us for a while. This wasn't the first time our home had opened its doors to someone in need, and it wouldn't be the last. For my mom, helping others was instinctual. Her warmth was a fundamental part of who she was; there was no question in her mind that this family should have a place to stay. Lisa was going through tough times, and her two sons, Jacob, a bit older than me, and Jeremiah, who was around my age, had become familiar faces in the neighborhood. I knew them almost like extended family, though we weren't truly related. I didn't mind sharing my space—that's what I initially told myself.

That evening, we all went about our usual routines, though the house felt fuller, filled with the sounds and presence of extra people. My mom prepared extra blankets and set up a place on the floor for the older boy, a makeshift bed, something she called a "pallet." It was her way of making guests comfortable in our modest home. There was a charm to it, a warm, thoughtful gesture from someone who had grown accustomed to making do with what she had. That was my mom's style—making room where there seemed to be none, creating warmth from simplicity. I'd grown used to it over the years, finding comfort in the idea that our home could expand and adapt to hold whoever needed it.

That night, I lay in bed, drifting to sleep under the comforting weight of blankets and the soft hum of the night outside. Jeremiah was beside me, his breathing slow and steady, already lost in his dreams. Jacob was on the floor nearby, wrapped in the cocoon of blankets my mom had set out. It felt safe, almost cozy, with the three of us in one room. I closed my eyes, letting the darkness pull me under, feeling that familiar sense of security in my own home.

But in the middle of the night, I was jolted awake. At first, it was just a faint awareness, that half-awake state where the line between dream and reality blurs. The room was cloaked in shadows, but the soft light from the illuminating parking lot outside filtered through the window, casting a gentle glow. I could see the outlines of Jeremiah in bed with his head turned away, facing my feet, and Jacob lying on the floor beside me. But then, I quickly became aware of something else—a touch. It was initially light and hesitant, almost as if testing to see if I would notice. But then it became more insistent, enough to pull me from sleep fully.

My heart pounded in my chest as I lay there, frozen and unsure of what was happening. The touch was strange and unfamiliar; as it lingered, I felt my skin prickle with unease. In the innocence of my young mind, I didn't have words for this, nor an understanding of why it felt wrong, only that it did. I stayed silent, caught between confusion and fear, not wanting to move or make a sound. It was as though a part of me hoped that if I stayed still long enough, the moment would end, and I could slip back into sleep and forget it had ever happened.

But the touch didn't stop, and I felt a wave of emotions I couldn't understand in that stillness. I lay there, every muscle tense, wishing I could escape without moving or confronting whatever this was. It was a strange, surreal experience to be awake in the dark, surrounded by the familiar yet feeling like a stranger in my room. The place that had always been a sanctuary now felt foreign, as though an invisible line had been crossed and a boundary breached.

Jacob's touch continued, subtle at first, nudging at the edge of my awareness and pulling me from the half-sleep I had drifted into. The room was quiet; the only sounds were the gentle rustle of fabric and the low murmur of his voice. I couldn't make out the words, but somehow the tone convinced me to slide off my bed and onto the floor. I was young, just old enough to begin carving out small, independent moments for myself, yet still unaware of the boundaries between trust and betrayal. Whatever was happening felt strange, but in my innocence, I wondered if maybe this was normal. Surely it had to be, I told myself, trying to quiet the stirring unease.

Realizing that my mom had carefully prepared the floor, I could trust him, right? She welcomed them into our home as I'd seen her do for others before—relatives and friends in need of a place to rest—and so the floor had always held a feeling of warmth, a sense of care stitched into its folds. But tonight, under the weight of what was unfolding, that familiar comfort began to slip away, replaced by a feeling of dread that settled heavily over me.

As I lay there, his voice softened, urging me closer until I found myself beside him. My head was swimming with half-formed questions I couldn't quite articulate: Is this how things should be? Should I be feeling this unsettled? But no answers came, only the lingering quiet of the room as Jacob gently tugged at the waistband of my pajamas, sliding them down and exposing me to the cool air. The bareness of my body was new and strange, making me feel both vulnerable and isolated in a way I'd never experienced.

I lay there, barely breathing, my thoughts racing as the night seemed to deepen around us. I knew something was off, but I didn't know how to name it or if it was something that could even be named. The trust I had instinctively given, the sense of safety my mom had so carefully nurtured, all seemed to dissolve in that space between us, replaced by a sharp, raw awareness that something irreversible was happening. "Ouch!" I projected, lying there motionless, not knowing what to do, but aware that whatever had been innocent and unspoiled within me had changed forever. I was no longer a virgin at the age of nine.

Finally, I managed to escape the vulnerability of being on the floor, my movements slow and quiet as I tiptoed to the bathroom down the hall. I closed the door behind me, feeling the cool floor beneath my feet, and stood there momentarily, breathing heavily. I could see my reflection in the bathroom mirror, the wide eyes of a boy who didn't fully understand what had just happened but knew it was something he didn't want to feel again. I splashed water on my face, hoping the cold would chase away the lingering sense of unease, of violation. But it didn't—it lingered, sinking deeper, settling into a nameless place inside me.

When I finally returned to bed, I lay there for the rest of the night, eyes wide open, watching the shadows shift with the first light of dawn. The world outside continued as normal, indifferent to the small, silent storm brewing within me. I kept it to myself, locking it away in a quiet corner of my mind, as if by hiding it there, I could pretend it hadn't happened. And so, it became a secret, a story I never shared with anyone, not even my mom. It's strange to reflect on it now, the way I instinctively knew to remain silent, to carry it alone.

Finding myself in a state of vulnerability and violation at such a young age shaped how I viewed the world. It was as if a crack had formed in the mirror of my innocence, and no matter how much time passed, I could never see myself—or others—in the same way again. Trust became complicated. Safety no longer felt guaranteed. And love... well, love began to resemble caution more than connection.

Twice it happened. Twice, my innocence was taken without permission. And though I wore my smile and maintained appearances, I carried the silence like a second skin. I often asked myself, Why me? Why did it happen again? Was there something about me—something I projected—that made people think it was okay to cross that line? Such questioning is dangerous because it tries to assign blame to the one who was harmed. But I didn't know that then. I just knew something inside me had shifted.

As I got older, I began building walls—strong ones. Walls made of sarcasm, humor, distance, and guarded smiles. They were my survival strategy. When you've been hurt secretly, you learn to protect yourself loudly. You learn how to be present without ever being fully exposed. Those walls weren't just about keeping people out; they were about keeping me in, securing me from the possibility of ever being hurt like that again.

In Oakland, those kinds of walls could mean everything. You see, in a city like ours, where Black boys are already targets, where poverty and proximity to pain can shape your entire destiny, having any emotional vulnerability can feel like a liability. We're not just navigating the streets—we're navigating trauma. And when you grow up without proper guidance or healing, those walls can turn into prisons. They don't just protect you—they keep you from ever feeling free.

And yet... there was something else that violation exposed me to: something I never expected—same-sex intimacy. I wouldn't even have had language for it back then. But those moments—dark and confusing as they were—opened a mental portal: a future that might be, a curiosity I didn't ask for. Over time, I questioned whether those thoughts would have existed if those events hadn't happened. It wasn't about desire, not then; it was about confusion, identity, and the shame of trying to make sense of a stolen experience that carried echoes into my adolescence and adulthood.

OAKLAND HILLS, MILWAUKEE RIVERS

I tried to bury it all. Packed the thoughts deep down beneath other things—school, relationships, faith, goals. I figured I would never have had to live it if I had never spoken it. But memories don't just disappear. They simmer. They whisper. And they wait for you in moments of stillness. Until one day, I decided not to suppress it anymore. I chose to face it, to give my thoughts a name, and to share them—but only with someone I believed would handle them delicately—someone who, even in my brokenness, I trusted to hold space for me.

But even then, my innocence and vulnerability were stolen once more. It was a cycle I never asked to be in, yet I found myself repeating it. And still, this is where grace entered. "How we move forward depends on our desire to stay bound or be liberated." That quote became a lifeline. I held onto it like breath.

Even in pain, we have a choice. We can allow the wounds to become our identity, or we can let them become our testimony. I chose the latter—not because it was easy, but because it was necessary. I could no longer afford to stay bound by shame, silence, and stolen power. Liberation required truth. And that truth was layered, messy, painful, and honest.

So, I say this now for anyone who has ever been violated, confused, or silenced—especially Black boys who never got to cry, who never got to speak, who had to become men before they were ready: your story doesn't end at the moment of your trauma.

I didn't let the events of Oakland define me or chain me. I chose to live. To love. To trust again—even if just in small ways. Because survival is only the beginning. Healing… that's the revolution.

However, just when I thought I had buried the weight of it all deep enough, life shook the ground beneath me again, revealing the cracks I never knew existed.

CHAPTER 05
Fault Lines

"Life is uncertain, and events unfold without warning. The key to survival lies in relying on what has been instilled in you, allowing it to surface as a form of protection when needed."

Sometimes, memories feel so vivid, as if they're unfolding in the present. They return, pulling us back to a moment with raw clarity that reawakens old feelings and, for a time, shifts our whole perspective. That's how it is every time I recall October 17, 1989. This memory, each time, feels like I'm right there again.

It was just an ordinary weekday evening in the Bay Area. People streamed out of work, spilling onto the streets, boarding buses, cars, and trains, and heading home after long, exhausting commutes. Many who worked in San Francisco lived on the outskirts, a couple of hours away. It was the price they paid to have a shot at that famed West Coast lifestyle—a dream that promised sun, opportunity, and a higher wage to match. But October 17th seemed to have different plans.

That day, I started my morning in Oakland as usual. I was staying with my Aunt Cheryl in Berkeley, and every morning, I'd catch the bus to Oakland for school. It wasn't the first time I'd stayed with her, as my mom and I went through some ups and downs, and my aunt's place had become my sanctuary. She did her best to create a stable environment for me, knowing I would eventually return to my mom. She didn't treat me like a guest but kept me on the same routines, providing a sense of consistency that I'd been missing. And for a child moving back and forth between two different worlds, that consistency felt like breath. Like an anchor.

When you're young and your reality is constantly shifting—different houses, different rules, different energy—you start to feel like the ground beneath you is always moving. It's hard to know where you stand when the expectations change depending on whose front door you walk through. But at her house, things didn't change. Bedtime stayed the same. Chores didn't skip. Meals were always at the table—not in front of the TV or eaten alone in a room. That rhythm became something I didn't even know I needed.

Because underneath all the movement—between city blocks and family dynamics, I truly craved something I could count on. Something that didn't seem temporary. Her steadiness provided that for me. In a world that often felt unpredictable, especially for a young Black boy learning to read faces and situations for survival, her consistency offered a kind of safety. It was a quiet reminder that I didn't have to earn love by performing or adapting—I could exist and still be cared for.

That kind of environment doesn't erase the instability, but it helps you survive it. It becomes a blueprint. A reference point for what stability could feel like. And later in life, when the ground started shaking again, I found myself searching for that same sense of rhythm—something, or someone, that felt like home.

So, just like every morning, I woke up around 5:30 a.m., with my Aunt Cheryl already getting ready for work. I went through my daily routine, waited for the bus, and went to school. It was my own way of coping, a kind of escape into the rhythm of everyday life—a chance to feel normal, no matter what.

When school let out that day, I made the hour-and-a-half journey back, navigating the transfer buses downtown and following my usual route to the house. It wasn't easy for a 10-year-old to commute like that, but it was my ritual, and I'd grown accustomed to it. Once home, I did what was expected of me: I sat down to do my homework. Math problems and vocabulary words were work I didn't particularly enjoy, but in elementary school, skipping wasn't an option.

At that time, my aunt was nearly finished with the renovations on the house. She added a lower level, expanding her cozy single-family home by including more bedrooms to accommodate people like me. In the meantime, the house sat securely on sturdy metal beams, precariously elevated above the foundation below as the work was completed. She wrapped entryways in thick plastic to keep out the dust, sealing off the construction areas from our living spaces. Living in a half-finished house was surreal, but for us, it was home.

That evening, my uncle Robert and aunt Georgia sat in the living room, probably watching the early evening news while I worked at the kitchen table. My little cousin, a three-year-old ball of energy with caramel skin, bright eyes, and a smile that could light up the whole room, was there too. She perched on a chair across from me, more interested in making me laugh than letting me get through my homework. Her tiny hands held onto the table as she wobbled back and forth in the chair, giggling and trying her hardest to get my attention.

Then, we felt a subtle tremor, barely noticeable at first. I remember thinking, "Was that an earthquake?" Little tremors were no surprise to us in California. We had them occasionally, and they were a part of life. But something about this one felt different. I glanced at my cousin, who was still laughing, blissfully unaware. My aunt and uncle's voices came from the other room, steady and calm. And then, it hit. The whole house lurched violently, swaying as if we were on a giant ship in rough waters. The ground shook so fiercely that I had to grab the table to steady myself, and my cousin's laughter turned to cries as the reality of what was happening sank in. The swaying intensified, each movement more jarring than the last, and in those seconds, I thought the whole house might come crashing down around us. It was more than an earthquake; it felt like the ground was rebelling.

My aunt and uncle yelled, "Get Michelle!" I scrambled to pull my cousin close. My mind was racing—hadn't they taught us in school what to do? Find a doorway, get under a table, and hold on tight. We practiced it in drills, but nothing had prepared me for the actual experience of a big earthquake. I found myself standing in the doorway, hoping it would be enough to protect us. The tremor lasted only seconds, but in the chaos, time stretched. It felt like an eternity before it finally stopped, leaving the house in an eerie, stunned silence.

* * *

When the shaking ended, the power was out. We stood there, gathering our wits, and stepped outside. The entire neighborhood seemed to have fallen silent, except for the wailing of car alarms, the crackle of broken glass underfoot, and the faint smell of smoke drifting nearby. Neighbors were outside too, their faces marked by the same dazed expressions. We had all come outside, half-afraid the ground might shake again.

The aftermath was chaotic, and the news came in pieces. We learned that one of the bridges had collapsed and that the freeway had crumbled in certain areas, trapping countless commuters in their cars—people who, like every other day, had been heading home to their families. The scenes on TV that evening were like nothing I'd ever seen: images of buildings engulfed in flames, streets lined with rubble, and firefighters racing to help those trapped.

The fear and uncertainty were unlike anything I had felt before, yet I felt lucky standing there with my uncle, aunt, and little cousin. We were shaken but safe, alive, holding on to each other as the sun set on a city that had changed forever. That day, I understood how quickly life could change, how the ground beneath us could shift without warning, leaving us to piece our lives back together in the aftermath. It was a lesson that even the most solid ground could betray you. However, at some point in time, you learn to rebuild anyway.

* * *

When Aunt Cheryl got home from work, she moved straight into action. I remember the sound of the front door opening and her voice calling my name urgently. "Where is he?" she asked, scanning the room until her eyes landed on me. Even though the shaking had stopped, her presence steadied something in me. She came from San Francisco—crossing the same bridge that collapsed—and still, her first concern was me. I'll never forget when she sat me down later that evening and said, "My concern is ensuring you are alright. Through all of this, although scary, I want you to know that I'm with you." That sentence stayed with me. I slept in her bed for the next few weeks—not because I had to, but because being close to her gave me the comfort that the ground had taken away..

For several nights, the aftershocks arrived like uninvited visitors in the dead of night, and small quakes lingered in our bones, serving as a haunting reminder of the earth's ferocity. Each one jolted us awake; some were more subtle, resembling a distant roll of thunder, while others were more violent, causing us to leap from bed as we braced for the worst. It felt as if the earth, unable to settle after the chaos of that initial quake, continued to tremble, sending wave after wave of aftershocks that shook our beds, knocked picture frames from walls, and prevented us from resting soundly.

Every time one struck, the memories of October 17th rushed back in a flash, vivid and raw. The momentary rumble took me back to that jarring movement, the fierce shaking that had upended our world. Each aftershock seemed to test the house, the foundations, and our nerves, making us wonder if another big quake was waiting just around the corner. I could see it in my aunt's face—the tautness, the lingering unease behind her eyes. She would check on us each night, ensuring everyone was safe, her footsteps soft but quick as she peered into our rooms.

Our neighborhood had changed as well. People moved with a new kind of caution, stepping lightly as if afraid their very footsteps might disturb the earth once more. Strangers exchanged glances of recognition and nods that conveyed, "We've been through it, we're still here." Every crack in the walls and every creak in the floorboards became amplified, feeding an ever-present anxiety that seemed to hum just beneath the surface.

And yet, we carried on, forging new routines out of the strange, fractured days. My aunt ensured the flashlights were easy to reach and the batteries were fresh; we left a few water jugs on the counters, just in case. I learned to recognize the low murmur of concern in the adults' conversations. Their words were muted yet laced with worry, always circling back to that day, to those we'd heard about who hadn't been so lucky, and to what might happen if the ground shifted again.

In those nights, sleep became light and broken, filled with the memory of the house moving as if it might fall apart, and how everything around us felt so weak, so close to collapsing. Each aftershock was a sharp reminder—like a jolt through the body—that we weren't safe yet. But somehow, those moments pulled us closer together, waiting side by side for the ground to stop shaking and for life to feel normal again.

Even after the shaking ended, something inside me didn't settle. It wasn't just the walls or the cracked streets—it was losing the feeling of safety I thought I had. That earthquake showed me that life can change quickly, without warning, and not everything will return to how it was. As a kid, that truth hit hard. I realized that the world isn't always steady, and you can't always count on things to remain the same.

And it wasn't just the fear of the ground shaking again—it was the fear of returning home and finding that nothing had changed. That the lights would still be off. That the moods in the room would shift faster than I could track. I'd have to be on edge, pretending everything was fine, to keep the peace. A part of me didn't want to return—not because I didn't love my mom, but because love doesn't always equal safety. Even at that young age, I was starting to understand the difference.

That began my journey of learning how to live with fear quietly. Even when I pretended to be okay, deep down I was still holding onto the anxiety that something else might break. That earthquake wasn't the only unstable aspect of my life. There were other types of aftershocks, too—arguments between adults, sudden relocations, changes I couldn't control. Each one made me feel unsteady, as if I had to be prepared for whatever came next.

I started paying closer attention to small things—creaks in the floor, flickers in the light, and the low rumble of buses that sometimes felt like the earth was stirring again. But the truth was, the tremors in my heart were just as constant. I never knew when the next argument would erupt, I might be sent away again, or a quiet day would become heavier. The earthquake didn't just train my body to react; it trained my mind to always be ready.

In Oakland, I had to learn to be alert. I didn't have the words back then, but I knew how to read the room and sense when something was off. I learned to hold my breath when things got tense, hide my fear, appear strong, and act as if everything didn't bother me. That's what surviving looked like—keeping everything inside, pretending everything was fine.

The earthquake revealed more than just how to endure a frightening moment and conceal my feelings; it enabled me to continue even when shaken inside. I became adept at putting on a smile, adhering to a routine, and holding myself together, even when nothing felt right.

That night, I remember whispering a prayer. Not a fancy one—just a simple, "God, please don't let it happen again." I didn't know how to pray like the grown-ups did. But I believed someone might be listening. That someone could hold what I didn't know how to name. Looking back, that might've been the first time I reached for faith—not because someone told me to, but because I needed to believe that someone had their hand on me when the world felt like it was spinning out of control.

That earthquake wasn't the first time the ground had fallen away beneath me. There would be other moments—less physical, but just as real—that would shake my world again. The moments that can't be fixed with flashlights or emergency kits. But somehow, I'd keep going. Because surviving the quake wasn't just about making it through—it was about learning how to live after the shaking stops.

And when you grow up in chaos, especially in a place like Oakland, you learn fast: either you cover up your cracks… or the world might break you open. But, some cracks stay hidden for years—until the ground shifts just enough to remind you they were always there.

CHAPTER 06
Cover-Ups

"You can take the time to cover up an imperfection, but at some point, it's going to reveal its flaws. You either own it or repeat the cycle."

Life was hard sometimes, harder than any kid would or should experience, but things happened. Sometimes it was no electricity, no food, too many unexpected visitors, or other unspoken struggles. I often covered up the challenges I faced by packing them away in my memory, hoping they would dissipate like steam into the cool air. As times got hard, so did my ability to remain at home.

I was experiencing another episode of staying with my Aunt Cheryl, seeking refuge from the chaos of my home life. My aunt was more than just family; she was an outlet, another mother figure, and a savior in the face of turmoil. Whenever tensions flared between my mom and aunt—often sparked by financial strain or unpredictable moments in our home—my aunt would step in, offering me a haven when I needed it most. During those days, the threat of Child Protective Services loomed large; the system was quick to intervene, snatching children away without regard for the stability of family connections. It was a harsh reality that made me sincerely appreciate the safe harbor my aunt provided.

Unfortunately, my mom's strength and resolve sometimes created a ripple between her and my aunt, a subtle tension that I witnessed repeatedly. It wasn't that my mom and aunt didn't love each other; rather, their bond was tested by the weight of differing perspectives. My aunt, ever the protector, often held a different view on how things should be done. She would challenge my mom's choices, perhaps out of concern or a deep-seated belief that there was a better way. My mom, however, had her convictions and was not easily swayed. She knew what she believed was best for me, and nothing—not even the well-meaning words of those closest to her—could change that.

I would sit quietly, watching two women who had been through so much together speak in soft tones that carried an edge that only those who love each other deeply can have. I could feel the weight of their unspoken words, the frustration bubbling beneath their voices, but neither would admit it. My mom, always confident in her decisions, would stand firm, declaring, "That's my son, I had him!" She said it not out of arrogance, but as an acknowledgment of choices made in the name of survival—choices that sometimes brought heartache. And for my aunt, that sometimes felt like an insurmountable wall.

What my aunt couldn't always understand was that my mom's "That's my son, I had him!" wasn't born out of defiance, but from a deeper place—a place of hurt and longing, shaped by years of yearning for the child she could never have. I was her miracle. Her blessing. The one who had come after eleven failed pregnancies. The one who had survived when so many others hadn't. I was her answered prayer, and every decision she made was filtered through that lens. She might have felt shame that her choices were not producing the best opportunity for me—her only son. Sometimes, I could hear my mom's voice crack when she spoke about how God had blessed her with me. She would reflect on those years—those painful years of loss, each miscarriage another wound she bore in silence. She had become accustomed to the emptiness that followed each failed attempt. Each time, she had to find the strength to pick herself up and try again, but that hope was dashed with every effort. Until, finally, there was me. I was the child who had made it and defied the odds.

My grandmother often referred to me as "the miracle child," her voice full of pride and reverence. She would tell the story of how my mom had nearly given up hope and how each pregnancy felt like a cruel reminder of what could never be. And yet, I had come. I was the one who survived, the one who made it out alive when so many others didn't. But despite being her miracle, life didn't make things easy for us. There were still the challenges of daily life, the struggles that didn't magically disappear just because I was born.

The world didn't pause for miracles. It was as if life had given her the most precious gift, only to remind her that no gift comes without its burdens. There was no instruction manual for how to raise a child who had been longed for, and no roadmap for navigating the complexities of being a mother after loss. As she navigated through motherhood, there were sometimes ripples in her relationships that were hard to smooth out. My aunt, the woman who had been raised alongside my mom, had a different kind of love that often clashed with my mom's more solitary resolve—a love that challenged her to do better by me and for me.

Settled into my aunt's home, a familiar rhythm of comfort enveloped me, and there was her bedroom. Located on the lower level at the back of her newly renovated house, it was a cozy sanctuary adorned with solid oak furniture that seemed to have its own weight and presence. The bed, with its grand footboard adorned with decorative towers, felt like a fortress to me. Back then, it was a statement of quality and comfort. My aunt worked long hours, which meant I often commandeered her room for my adventures, sprawled out with the TV blaring music videos on BET. It was my little kingdom, a space where my imagination could run wild. I was often mesmerized by the fact that her bedroom had its own bathroom. Back then, no one I knew had an ensuite—it felt like pure luxury to me.

That day, I felt particularly inspired. My mind was alight with visions of being a ninja sword fighter, channeling the spirit of the Teenage Mutant Ninja Turtles. I found a knife—about fourteen inches long, with a blade that gleamed as I whipped it back and forth, thrusting it as if battling an evil villain. But then, in the heat of my imagination, disaster struck. The knife met the dresser, and I watched in horror as a sizable chunk of wood flew off, landing on the floor with a thud. Panic coursed through me. There was no way my aunt wouldn't notice the damage; it was too significant to hide.

In a frenzy of desperation, I scanned the room and caught sight of my aunt's makeup, her routine in preparing for work each morning. I grabbed it and frantically tried to cover the exposed wood, convinced that my quick fix would be enough to mask my blunder. Hours passed, and eventually, the door swung open as my aunt returned from a day at work. She walked in, and I knew my ruse was in jeopardy. Her eyes locked onto the damaged dresser, and without missing a beat, she asked, "What happened to my dresser?"

I faced a crossroads at that moment: Should I lie to protect myself, tell the truth, or own up to my mistake? The weight of my decision pressed down on me. I opted for honesty, my voice trembling as I explained it was an accident. But the truth didn't shield me from the inevitable; I had crossed a line, and I was met with a punishment that was both deserved and humbling.

But the truth is, I had been covering up long before the makeup ever touched the dresser. That moment wasn't just about hiding a scratch in the wood—it was about masking all the other things I couldn't name: the hurt, the confusion, the fear of never being enough. In homes where survival was the priority, covering up wasn't just something we did; it became who we were.

I learned early that sometimes it was easier to pretend than to explain, smile than cry, and act like I understood things I didn't, just so no one would see how lost I felt. That dresser, broken and disguised, symbolized how we all can walk through life—with patched hearts and painted-over cracks, hoping nobody will look too closely.

In many ways, the punishment I received that day didn't sting because of the belt; it stung because I had hoped that telling the truth might spare me. But even in that, I learned: telling the truth doesn't always mean you'll be protected. And so, I carried that lesson forward—not just in behavior, but in belief. I began to guard my feelings like I tried to cover that dresser—quickly, quietly, while hoping the flaws wouldn't show.

Because in our house, and in homes like mine all across Oakland, emotions weren't always allowed to take up space. You learned to be tough. You learned to be still. And most of all, you learned to survive the best way you could, even if that meant hiding your truth. Emotional cover-ups became the unspoken rule—no one said it aloud, but we all knew the cost of being too honest, open, and raw.

What started as hiding mistakes transformed into hiding pain. What began with fear of punishment evolved into fear of judgment, rejection, and misunderstanding. Over time, that fear became familiar. It taught me how to shape-shift to fit into the rooms I entered: to shrink when I felt too visible, and to harden when I felt too exposed.

That's what survival looked like. That's what we knew. But at some point, I had to reckon with this truth: You can take the time to cover up an imperfection, but eventually, it will reveal its flaws. You either own it or repeat the cycle.

And that's the choice I would keep facing—repeatedly—as the cracks beneath me kept shifting, daring me to patch them once more or finally confront what was broken.

When the ground beneath you cracks, something inside you shifts as well. You don't just pick up the broken pieces; you carry them. You learn quickly that survival is more than finding a new place to live; it's about building a new version of yourself within that unfamiliar space.

At the time, I thought Aunt Cheryl was the only one who could ever offer me that kind of covering. But life would later show me that some coverings are generational, and I would come to know another woman who carried that same strength in silence.

Every move to a different house, every new bedroom, every new face at the dinner table plants seeds. Some seeds take root; others rot where they fall. But the truth is, even the best soil can't erase the memory of the last thing I had to cover up. And so, you grow crooked sometimes, fragile often. But still, you grow.

RESTLESS SOIL

"You can plant new seeds and still feel the sting of the soil you came from."

There are moments when life invites you into something new—but doesn't allow you time to heal from the past. This section is about transitions: not the smooth kind, but the ones that yank you from one place and drop you in another, expecting you to bloom.

These chapters reveal what it means to search for identity among cities, among relatives, among versions of yourself. In Milwaukee, I discovered cousins who became like siblings. I experienced laughter and new rules. But I also encountered the haunting echo of wounds I hadn't yet named.

Even when things improved, my past never let go easily. I was still tethered to memories, questioning whether I could be whole in a place that didn't know my entire story. And yet—I kept growing. Bent, sometimes. Scarred, often. But still reaching toward the light.

This is the span between running from something and running to something, unaware of the difference.

CHAPTER 07
Cartoons, Cousins, and Crossroads

"Life often brings countless moments where "no" seems to be the only answer, but everything can change when you finally hear "yes" from the right person. It can change the entire trajectory of your life."

Saturday mornings were sacred. It was the one day kids across the neighborhood could be found glued to their favorite cartoons—an unspoken ritual to unwind from the long school week. For me, that ritual meant He-Man. I watched in awe as he lifted his sword to the sky, summoning power from above with a fierce, electrifying "By the power of Grayskull!" The lightning struck him in glorious arcs, infusing him with unimaginable strength, transforming him and his skittish feline companion into defenders of the universe. In those moments, sitting cross-legged in front of my small black-and-white TV, I felt like I was right there with him, as if his power were my power too.

I watched alone in my room, which, although small and mostly empty, felt like my sanctuary. My bed and the crate holding my TV were the only furnishings, and the walls, free of decorations or clutter, seemed to wrap around me like a protective cocoon. A little light crept in through the shade, giving the room a dusky glow that felt perfect for tuning out the world. I could hear other kids playing outside, their laughter mixing with the faint hum of cars and city sounds, but inside my room, it was quiet—just me and my cartoons, a space where I could lose myself every Saturday morning.

But that particular Saturday, things changed. The family was in town visiting from Milwaukee, bouncing between the houses of aunts and uncles scattered around the Bay Area. Back then, staying connected was different. We didn't have cell phones, and even calling long distance on the home phone was a planned expense, so we saved those special "catch-up" moments for in-person visits, letters, or the occasional, much-anticipated long-distance call. That morning, while I was in my room, my mom was in the living room when we heard a knock on the door. My heart leaped a little at the sound of visitors.

It was my Aunt Grace from Milwaukee visiting my mom. She'd been staying with relatives in Berkeley, but now it was our turn to host. I remember hearing her voice before I saw her—a rich, warm tone that instantly transported me back to the last time I'd seen her, maybe years before, at my grandmother's funeral. When she finally came into view, she looked just as I remembered: standing about 5'7" with a radiant caramel complexion. Her hair was styled in a neat jerry curl that bounced lightly with each movement, framing her face with glamour. She was dressed like she'd been waiting all week for this visit, her cheeks glowing with a soft, rosy flush and her two gold teeth catching the light when she smiled. Aunt Grace was the kind of woman who, just by entering a room, filled it with warmth. She made you feel like she was hugging you, even before her arms reached out.

My mom and Aunt Grace settled into the living room, their voices a familiar background hum. Back then, there was an unbreakable rule: "Stay in a kid's place." It was drilled into us that children didn't meddle in adult conversations. As curious as I was, I kept my place on the floor, content to watch cartoons, while still catching fragments of their laughter and chatter through the walls. At one point, I heard Aunt Grace ask, "Where's my nephew?" My ears perked up, knowing I might be summoned at any moment, so I kept an ear out, half hoping she'd peek into my room.

And soon enough, there she was in the doorway. I glanced up, a grin spreading across my face as I jumped up from the floor to greet her with a hug. For a moment, the cartoons disappeared, the little black-and-white TV, the dark room— all of it faded as she enveloped me in one of her signature hugs—warm and grounding. Even as my oldest aunt, seeing her, especially after she traveled so far, made me feel special, like I was her favorite nephew.

That spring, my aunt invited me to spend the summer with her in Milwaukee. The invitation was thrilling; it offered the chance to travel alone and explore a whole new world. I had flown solo before, to Arkansas to visit my grandmother, but Milwaukee felt like a grand adventure—a place I had only ever heard about in family stories. My mom took me shopping for a few new things: a pair of jeans, some T-shirts, and a pair of stonewashed red overalls, the very first "cool" piece of clothing I'd ever owned.

The overalls hung loosely on me, making my skinny frame feel cool for once. I weighed about 180 pounds and stood close to six feet tall. For some reason, the overalls gave me a sense of energy and confidence. They ended just above my shoes with a slight roll resting on top, adding a touch of style. The pockets were deep, perfect for storing all the quarters I'd collected from the nearby laundromat. This time, the clothes brought me joy and made me feel like I finally "fit in" with my peers. I couldn't wait to wear them in Milwaukee and look the part.

* * *

The day arrived, and my mom dropped me off at the airport, ensuring the flight attendants would look out for me. I remember boarding the plane and feeling the excitement build—the thrill of traveling across the country. When we touched down at Chicago's O'Hare Airport, Aunt Grace was waiting, her smile as big and bright as ever. She grabbed my bags and ushered me to her van—a massive blue beast that felt more like a moving living room. Inside, it was carpeted from floor to ceiling, with dark blue bucket seats and a long back seat, all covered in plush fabric. I had never seen anything like it; it felt like I was riding in luxury, a space large enough for our whole summer together.

After an hour's drive, we arrived at her house in Milwaukee, where I was greeted by a scene straight out of a dream. Kids were everywhere—cousins who felt like instant friends, riding bikes, running through the yard, and jumping over banisters as if the place were a kid's playground. Aunt Grace beamed at me and announced, "Keyimani, these are all your cousins." My jaw practically dropped. It was like walking into a family reunion, but this was every day, all summer long.

That summer was a whirlwind of laughter and adventure. There were fishing trips, afternoons at the park, church services on Sundays, and, on special days, outings with my older cousins. I tagged along as much as possible, a little tagalong shadow eager to see the city, learn their stories, and be part of their world. They'd smile when I asked, "Can I come?" and wave me along, never turning me away, allowing me to feel like I was one of them.

As summer progressed, I began to feel more at home. My cousins became like siblings, and bonds formed that went beyond family into something deeper. As the final weeks of summer approached, I dreaded leaving. I felt a strong desire to stay, to make this place home in a way I hadn't anticipated. During one of my calls back home, I told my mom just how much fun I was having, and then I asked, "Can I stay?" The question hung in the air, and for a moment, I thought she hadn't heard me. There was a long pause, a silence I wasn't expecting, and a soft, measured "I'll think about it." I could tell she was weighing her thoughts, picturing her son 2,000 miles away, trying to imagine what that meant for both of us.

Weeks later, after much consideration and a heartfelt talk with Aunt Grace and my mom, "I'll think about it" turned into a "yes." Just like that, my world shifted. What had started as a summer trip became a new chapter: a life in Milwaukee where cousins were like siblings, family everywhere, and I found myself in a place I could call home. For that young Black boy from Oakland, that moment was the beginning of something bigger—a life built on family, love, and the bonds that held us all together across distance and time.

* * *

Life often brings countless moments when "no" seems to be the only answer, but everything can change when you finally hear "yes" from the right person. It can alter the entire trajectory of your life. My Mom's yes wasn't just a word—it was a door opening. A rescue wrapped in routine. A way out of something no one wanted to name fully.

What I didn't know then—but would come to understand years later—was that behind the scenes, there were quiet conversations that shaped this turning point. Aunt Grace didn't make that decision alone; she had talked with Aunt Cheryl, and both of them, in their own way, had seen enough. They recognized the patterns, the strain, the weight I was carrying as a child trying to adapt to a situation that wasn't always stable. It wasn't judgment—it was concern. It was protection. It was love that showed up uninvited but right on time.

My mother, though, has often shared her pain around that moment. Not the moment of letting me go, but how it felt for me not to be physically there. As if the choice were made for her, rather than with her. As if two of her sisters had conspired to remove her only child from her arms, from her care. I understand that now, in a way, I didn't back then. The regret she carried wasn't just about the distance but about feeling like she failed me, even when I never saw it that way. It's the kind of regret that settles in your bones, especially when you're a mother trying to do your best with limited options due to substance abuse and even less grace from the world around you.

But the truth is, I was caught between two kinds of love—one fighting to hold on and one stepping in to support me. Aunt Grace saw where the road I was on could lead. The world has a way of swallowing boys like me—boys with imagination, boys with too much freedom and not enough direction, boys who were trying to grow roots in soil that kept shifting beneath their feet. She wasn't trying to take me away to hurt my mom; she was trying to keep me from becoming another statistic. Another young Black boy lost to the streets, to the system, to silence. For that, I respected and shared every moment I got to uplift my mom's spirits as an assurance that God doesn't make mistakes. We were fortunate that it was part of the plan.

OAKLAND HILLS, MILWAUKEE RIVERS

That moment when a summer trip turned into a new life wasn't just a change of scenery; it was a quiet rescue—one that, in some ways, saved me. And yet it came with a cost: a separation that left its mark on all of us—my mom, my aunts, and me. It was the beginning of my physical escape, yes, but it also opened a deeper wound I'd carry for years: the guilt of asking to leave, the ache of being loved in different ways by different women, and the unspoken truth that sometimes survival means leaving parts of yourself behind.

CHAPTER 08
Seasons of Change

"There comes a moment when we need to pause, reflect, and recognize that life, even in its challenges, could be much harder. Be grateful."

It was my first year here, and I was still finding my way around the rhythm of the Midwest. The pace was different—slower and less crowded than the constant bustle of the Bay Area. It had a serene, almost gentle quality, as if the city itself was giving me room to breathe. I welcomed it. People were friendly in that open, easy way I hadn't experienced back home. My Aunt Grace had already managed the major task of getting me enrolled in school. It was late in the process to secure a spot so close to the school year, but she worked her magic, and I found myself set to start sixth grade at Walt Whitman Elementary, way on the south side of Milwaukee.

Leaving summer behind for school was hard, especially after a summer like that. There were months of bonding with my cousins and countless fishing trips with my aunt. Fishing was serious business in our family. Almost every day, except Sundays, we'd pile into my aunt's big, blue van, stocked with everything we needed: rods, tackle boxes, coolers, and snacks from Aldi's. Sundays were reserved for church; no fishing allowed, according to my aunt.

She held firmly to the belief that fishing on Sunday brought bad luck, and not even her deep love for it could sway her.

Each trip was an adventure. We drove all over Wisconsin, visiting lakes and rivers, often so loaded with fish by the end of the day that the coolers could barely close. We had our strategies, too—more kids meant more lines in the water and more fish on the way home. Sometimes, a game warden would show up, and there was always the thrill of claiming each kid had caught their full limit. And all of us could; fishing wasn't just a pastime. It was a requirement, a skill that had been passed down. By the time kids were old enough to hold rods, they knew how to bait hooks, reel in fish, unhook them, and clean them. It was a remarkable experience, one of which I was proud. Being part of a family that could fill buckets with fish and then gather around for a feast was something I had never experienced before, even though I grew up in the Bay Area around the ocean that held millions of fish.

When we got back from those long days, the ritual began. We'd unpack the van, setting up in the backyard or sometimes even in the kitchen, scaling panfish or skinning catfish, whatever had taken our bait. Nothing went to waste. "If it's big enough to bite, it's big enough to eat," the adults would say, grinning as they wrapped the smaller catches of illegally sized fish, like largemouth bass, in cloth or tucked them into plastic bags for the freezer. After the work was done, we'd scrub ourselves clean from a day of fish scales, lake water, and dirt. Then, we'd sit down for the real prize: fresh fried fish, still steaming from the oil, seasoned with Lawry's seasoning salt and black pepper, maybe even a splash of Red Hot for those who dared, and some freshly squeezed lemon. That taste—it was family, it was tradition, and it was summer itself.

But as the school year started, my life took on new routines. This time, I didn't need to navigate the city bus on my own. Instead, I waited for the yellow school bus that picked me up at the corner each morning at 6:45 am sharp. We all knew where each friend got on and off, and the rides were filled with laughter and chatter about what the day ahead might hold. At school, there was no room to slack; my mom had instilled in me the value of good grades, and the idea of disappointing her hung in the background, an unspoken motivator. I even became a crossing cadet, a duty I'd loved back in Oakland. Wearing that bright orange sash, gripping the stop sign, and halting traffic for my classmates gave me a rare taste of authority. For a few minutes, I had control over something as big as the street, and I cherished every moment.

Then, as fall deepened, I was introduced to my first Midwest winter. Wisconsin's cold was unlike anything I had ever experienced. In California, sixty degrees felt chilly enough for a coat. Now, I was bracing for temperatures that dipped below freezing, something I had only read about.

One day, while I was in class, the first snow began to fall. I was transfixed, watching as the delicate flakes drifted down like a fine, soft dusting of sugar. The sidewalks, the trees—everything outside became blanketed in white. For someone who had never seen snow, it was like stepping into a different world, one I had only imagined. It was beautiful and surreal, and it filled me with a strange thrill—a reminder of how life can surprise us when we least expect it. Milwaukee was turning out to be full of such surprises, pulling me deeper into experiences that I never would have had if I'd stayed back home.

But things began to change just as I started to feel rooted and see Milwaukee as something more than a temporary stop. Rumors floated through the air, whispering of a return to California. When I thought I had found my footing, I was being called back to where it all began. It was a bittersweet tug, and although I knew this wouldn't be the last time life would pull me in unexpected directions, leaving was never easy.

It wasn't just the idea of going back to Oakland that made me nervous—it was the fear that everything I had just started to build might fall apart. For the first time in a long time, I felt like I was growing. I wasn't just trying to survive anymore; I was starting to feel like I belonged, like I had a place, a routine, a future I could picture.

The thought of leaving made all of that feel shaky again. I wondered: If I return, will I lose this version of me? Will I still be able to grow the way I have here? Or will I slip back into the same old patterns I worked so hard to escape?

Aunt Grace didn't try to convince me to stay with long talks or heavy rules. However, I could feel her attempting to hold on in quiet ways. She made my favorite meals more frequently, checked in more often, and gave me hugs that lasted a few seconds longer. She was doing what she always did by showing me love without making it loud. All this was to prepare her heart just in case I had to go, even if she hoped I wouldn't.

That season taught me something significant: growth doesn't always come with grand moments or loud victories. Sometimes, it's about showing up every day and choosing to try again. It's about building something steady even when the future feels uncertain. Milwaukee allowed me to breathe and envision who I could become, not just who I had been. I didn't realize it then, but I was beginning to understand that true stability isn't solely about the location—it's about how deeply you feel seen, safe, and cared for while you're there.

And with all the change, all the questions, and all the uncertainty, one truth began to rise to the surface: There comes a moment when we need to pause, reflect, and recognize that life, even in its challenges, could be much harder. This didn't mean pretending everything was perfect—it meant learning to notice the small ways life was improving, even if I didn't know what tomorrow would bring.

CHAPTER 09
Between Homes

"Let yesterday guide the shaping of a better today. Let today lay the foundation for a brighter tomorrow. And let tomorrow spark aspirations that lead to your destiny."

Back in Oakland once again. By this time, we had moved three times, each relocation bringing new challenges. Life was always shifting beneath my feet, and with each move, I had to leave friends behind, figure out new schools, and adapt to fresh routines. These moves became a rhythm I had to learn—letting go, starting over, and finding ways to cope with the changes in between.

One of those moves placed us across from Highland Hospital. Living there, I witnessed things a kid my age probably shouldn't have been exposed to. Like clockwork, our small apartment became a revolving door every first and fifteenth of the month. Men would come and go, exchanging small packages of drugs for money from my mom's welfare check. It was an unspoken routine, but it was routine, nonetheless. Her need persisted when the money was gone, and I didn't always know how she managed to find her "fix." Maybe she had a tab with the dealer or used other methods, but somehow, she always got what she wanted. I never asked. I just saw, and in seeing, I grew up fast.

Life in Oakland wasn't easy, and I knew it. But in those moments of survival, things still brought a smile to my face, small pockets of normalcy that reminded me that life was more than just the struggle. Even as a single parent, my mom did her best to shield me from the hardest edges of her world, even though I could see the cracks in that shield. I knew she wanted the best for me, and even when money was tight, she always managed to keep a roof over our heads. I'll admit, electricity was a different story. PG&E, notorious for cutting off power when payments were overdue, didn't play around, and it wasn't uncommon to see electrical cords snaking across the walls outside, connecting one apartment to the next. Neighbors shared power when the bills piled up, looking out for one another in ways that felt both practical and quietly heroic. And on the nights when we were one of those families, we got by.

When returning from Milwaukee, I was greeted with a new place to stay. This next move took us from the semi-comfortable East 27th Street area into the heart of East Oakland, landing us on Seminary Avenue. My mom had moved there when I was away. It was her way of demonstrating that she was getting things and herself together. Seminary wasn't just any street; it was a part of town with a reputation. A bad one. People knew it as a place where drugs and danger met, where safety was never a given, and survival was the rule. This was no "white picket fence" kind of neighborhood, but it was our neighborhood now, and like everywhere else, we made it work. I figured maybe we moved because the rent got too high, or perhaps the landlord had had enough of our situation. Whatever the reason, here we were, in a place known for landmarks like the Fruitvale BART Station, the iconic International Boulevard that stretched into San Leandro, and blocks dotted with liquor stores, tire shops, and check-cashing places. The streets bustled with people from every walk of life—Black, Asian, Hispanic, all mingling together in a harmony that was rough around the edges but somehow held firm. The white folks lived further up, in the Oakland hills, but every now and then, you'd see one or two who hadn't made it out of this part of town, caught by the cost of California living like the rest of us.

I was wrapping up my last year of elementary school, the second semester of sixth grade, and had enrolled in Havenscourt, a middle school for grades

6-8, after being pulled out of school for my journey back to Oakland. Havenscourt was just a short walk from our place on Seminary, which I appreciated. This house was close to a bus station where buses roared to life in the early mornings, spreading out over Oakland and its winding streets to take people to work, school, or wherever the day needed them to be. Our apartment, a squat, stucco duplex painted a dull pink, sat halfway down the block, and from the street, it was nothing special. The building had a sturdy set of concrete steps leading to a second-floor patio that stretched outside our front door, with the stairs held up by steel poles that had a retro look straight out of the '70s. The inside was simple: a living room connected to a small kitchen on the right, my mom's bedroom straight ahead, a bathroom off the kitchen, and my bedroom off to the side.

We didn't have much furniture, but what we had was ours, well-traveled with us through all of our moves. The living room included a couch, a single chair, and a scratched-up coffee table, which was enough for us. My room featured a twin bed that sat squarely in the middle of the floor and a tiny 12-inch black-and-white TV balanced on top of an old blue milk crate. I didn't have a dresser, just a small closet with a few clothes hanging inside, but it was my space, my little corner of stability in a world that was always shifting.

Each morning, I walked the mile to Havenscourt. I didn't mind walking alone; I was used to it by then. Havenscourt had the typical setup for a California school—classrooms spread between a main building and trailers that stood as permanent fixtures on the blacktop. California schools had this charm, even when pieced together like that, and I liked it well enough. Making friends was easy; kids in Oakland were as familiar with change as I was, so friendships sparked quickly. Some days, my friends and I would hang out after school, maybe heading to one of our houses to play Atari or Nintendo.

One afternoon, I invited my friend over to play video games after school. We strolled back to my apartment, talking about our day—the teachers, the homework, and the funny things that happened at lunch. I had a key around my neck, held on a beaded chain like the ones on ceiling fans, with a little metal clamp at the end. My mom trusted me with it, and each day I'd pray I wouldn't lose it, knowing the trouble I'd be in if I did. As we climbed the steps to our apartment, I fished out the key, popped it into the lock, and turned the knob.

Inside, it was dim, and I automatically reached for the light switch. But when I flipped it, nothing happened.

Click. Click.

Darkness.

My heart sank. "Not again," I thought.

The electricity was off, and I knew what that meant. My mom had probably gone out to scrape together enough money to pay the bill so we could get the lights turned back on. I felt embarrassed, especially with my friend standing beside me. The shame of knowing our power was off hit hard, and I avoided his gaze, pretending it was no big deal. I'd been through it enough times to know the drill, but it was still a reminder of how precarious our situation was.

In that apartment, I learned to appreciate the small things. I remember pea soup becoming a staple meal—a cheap way to stretch food when things got tough. Each day felt like a struggle, but at least it was one I knew, a rhythm of ups and downs that kept us going. And now, my new friends at school, the ones I'd tried to shield from the reality of my life, were starting to see it too. Life on Seminary Avenue was hard, but it was mine, a chapter in a story I was beginning to understand. A chapter that revealed again that things were not good.

* * *

Later that year, the weight of everything I had been carrying intensified. Life had a way of pulling me in different directions, none of which seemed to lead anywhere better. As if the universe had deemed it time for another chapter of uncertainty, I was back in Milwaukee at the start of the school year, facing the daunting reality of entering the seventh grade. Edison Middle School was now the place where I would attempt to find some semblance of normalcy, but the truth was, nothing felt normal anymore.

The first semester had its moments of peace. There was a small comfort in being just down the street from my cousin's house, a familiar place where I could find solace. We spent countless hours together after I got out of school before walking back home—playing basketball in the backyard, talking about anything and everything, sharing laughs, and for a moment, I could pretend that the turmoil swirling around me didn't exist. My cousins were like a rock, an anchor in a sea of instability. Those were the moments when I felt like I could breathe again, as if life had stopped being so heavy.

I attempted to hold on to the promises of yesterday—the assurances of stability—but I always seemed to remain right in the middle. I knew there had to be some form of hope out there. So, I grounded myself in this thought: 'Let yesterday guide the shaping of a better today. Let today lay the foundation for a brighter tomorrow. And let tomorrow spark aspirations that lead to your destiny." That became more than a quote; it was a quiet truth I carried through every move, every classroom, and every street I learned to walk with caution. My yesterdays had shown me pain, but they also revealed resilience, allowing me to dream and hold on to the optimism of tomorrow.

That fleeting desire to dream—to imagine even a sliver of stability—was just an illusion, quickly shattered by life's relentless lessons. Lessons that didn't comfort, but carved into me a single, unforgiving truth: survival.

CHAPTER 10
Survival

"Life teaches us to adapt to situations, hardships, and problems with the hope that we will someday emerge as survivors."

After the first semester, everything shifted again. The call came, and just like that, my life was uprooted. I was headed back to Oakland—a place that held pain and belonging. But this time, it was a different side of town, with new challenges. By now, I knew the drill—pack, adapt, show up. But each move asked me to leave behind a growing version of myself.

I started laughing more and breathing deeper, trusting that stillness could last. But being sent back felt like folding away that boy—the one who was healing—to survive the shadows I knew all too well. Oakland didn't let you ease in. It made you re-learn how to speak, walk, and guard your heart. And I did, because I had to.

The hardest part wasn't just the streets or the expectations. It was what I carried inside—the version of me I couldn't show. I didn't have the words for it back then, but I knew how being in Oakland would impact me. I was starting to master learning how to smile through silence. But as the plane touched down in Oakland, I knew escaping reality wasn't an option. There was no outrunning the situations it would present or the memories it would resurface. All I could do was face it head-on and hope that, one day, it would all make sense.

I was used to it by now. Used to life pulling me in different directions, none of which seemed to lead anywhere better when I came back to Oakland. I was never in one place long enough to fully plant roots, and each move seemed to ask me to become someone slightly different—stronger, quieter, more alert, and less trusting. Somewhere in all those shifts, I wasn't just between homes—I was between selves. Between thriving and surviving.

Even when I didn't fully see it, people like Aunt Grace held space for me—staying connected without disrupting what I needed to navigate on my own. But space doesn't always mean safety. Sometimes it's just a wider room to carry the same weight.

I didn't know it then, but survival doesn't just mold you—it conceals you. It teaches you how to blend in, retreat behind silence, and tuck away dreams that don't feel safe anymore. That's what Oakland did to me—it dimmed the light that had just begun flickering in Milwaukee.

Each time I left Milwaukee, I left behind a version of myself that was beginning to grow. I was learning to breathe deeper, laugh louder, and trust the quiet rhythm of a more stable life. But each time I returned to Oakland, I had to put pieces of that boy away, tucking him behind a mask to get by. It was like folding away my own light, piece by piece, to survive.

When I was removed from Oakland, there were things I didn't have to think about, people I didn't have to face, and feelings I didn't have to embrace. There was a version of me I could ignore. The hidden one. The one that rested in silent shadows, waiting for the sun to come out just long enough to feel seen, only to vanish again when it went down. I didn't know how to speak about that version of me, not then. I just knew that being back in Oakland meant stepping into a space where I had to silence parts of myself, where I had to move differently, talk differently, and feel less—just to be okay.

Some aspects of that environment weren't good for me, but no one could see it. And I couldn't find the words or the courage to express it. Sometimes, when the pain becomes familiar, you stop calling it pain. You call it life. Thus, I kept the truth hidden, tucked behind my silence, layered in smiles that carried the weight of what I couldn't explain.

I didn't have the words then, but I wasn't quite the boy I used to be, and not yet the young man I was becoming. Just suspended somewhere in the middle, like the matrix, trying to find home and hoping someone would notice I was still there—still trying. I might have been too soft for the streets, too guarded for full connection, or too alert ever fully to rest. During these transitions, I wasn't just packing bags; I was learning how to carry my entire life in a way that didn't show how heavy it was.

You see, when you're surviving, you're not who you were and are not quite who you're becoming. You're in the middle, figuring it out, hoping the ground doesn't shift beneath you again before you can stand still. But I began to realize something: the in-between isn't just about survival; it's about shaping who I was meant to become, which is what I held on to.

I was maturing and learning, not only how to navigate change but also how to endure the emotional toll of constantly shapeshifting. To mask who I was, to escape reality. That lesson would prove even more significant in the years to come, especially when I would find myself at another crossroads—between love and expectation, between hiding and healing, and between silence and truth. It all contributed to my quest for freedom. Because freedom loses its flavor when you're still tasting the residue of bondage. And bondage keeps its strength when you're trying to survive.

CHAPTER 11
A Taste of Freedom

"Freedom loses its flavor when you're still tasting the residue of bondage. And bondage keeps its strength when you're trying to survive."

Transitions, especially for kids, are like a storm—unpredictable and often unsettling. And I was still carrying a version of myself I couldn't name—one shaped by silence, shadowed by fear, and too fragile for the kind of freedom I thought I was walking into.

It was the start of the second semester of seventh grade, and my life was about to change again. My mom, in a more stable place, had decided it was time for me to come back to Oakland and live with her. When my parents reunited, it stirred a hope I wasn't ready to name—a fragile belief that maybe this time we could become what we never were: a family under one roof. Still, I felt it. After so many years of bouncing between addresses and households, between cities and zip codes, this was the closest thing to the dream of stability I'd ever been offered.

After a few conversations with my mom and Aunt Grace, they decided I would return 'home' after finishing the fall semester in Milwaukee. I didn't realize it then, but Aunt Grace's influence was already beginning to shape the trajectory of my life—even from the sidelines. Even though I knew the streets, I didn't see the life I was walking back into. Oakland was the same—but I wasn't. I held on to this fragile hope: maybe we'd be a family this time. Perhaps this time, I'd get to stop searching for belonging and start building it.

When my mom met me at the airport, we drove back to what would become my new residence. Since she didn't have a car, she arranged for a friend to give her a ride to pick me up from the airport. As we pulled up to a busy street, she waved goodbye. I stepped out, feeling the cool California air against my skin, carrying both familiarity and something unknown, scanning around to see where "home" would be. We were on San Pablo Avenue, a busy, sprawling street lined with storefronts, small offices, churches, and the occasional rundown motel. I searched my surroundings for anything that resembled home—a house, an apartment, something. But all I saw were buildings and motels, places where people came and went. Where was the neighborhood, the place we'd live?

Alford, K. (2024). *Hotel Life* [Photograph]. Oakland, California: Keywords Unlocked, LLC

When I asked my mom where we were going, she pointed across the street to a worn-down motel. At first, I thought she was joking. But as we crossed the street and she led the way toward the office, the truth settled in, and my heart sank. This was it? My chest tightened with disappointment. It wasn't the homecoming I had envisioned in my mind. Not even close.

Just days ago, I was in Milwaukee, living in a five-bedroom house filled with warmth and laughter. It had a big kitchen that smelled like Saturday mornings, a dining room where we shared meals, and a basement where my cousins and I played as if the world outside didn't exist. That was a home—a place held together not just by walls but by people—especially her.

Aunt Grace had a way of making stillness feel safe. With her, love didn't have to be earned or explained. I didn't fully understand it then, but now I realize what I left behind wasn't just comfort—it was covering.

This? This felt like a step backward. I didn't say anything, though. I had learned how to tuck my feelings away, how to wear a mask when the truth felt too heavy. I told myself I should be grateful—I was here with my mom, and that was supposed to be enough. But deep down, I couldn't ignore the ache that whispered, this isn't what I hoped for. This isn't what I needed.

I returned to California, hoping—praying—that this move meant something had truly changed, that life with both of my parents meant we would finally be okay. But standing across from that motel, I realized I had mistaken presence for progress.

This wasn't a step forward. It felt like a step further into uncertainty. I didn't understand it. Why would she bring me back here, to this? If she didn't have things in order, if life was still this fragile, why not let me stay where I was safe, where I was supported, where I was finally starting to grow? In that moment, it didn't feel like love—it felt like loss. A loss of trust. A loss of stability. A loss of the small peace I had found just a few months earlier.

Maybe she thought having me near would fix what was broken. Maybe she missed me. But bringing me back before she was truly ready–before we were ready–didn't improve anything. It made things harder. It stirred up emotions that were already layered deep within me: confusion, frustration, and a quiet shame I couldn't quite shake. I had friends back in Milwaukee who would be heading into their spring semester with new clothes, warm homes, and a routine they could count on, but mine seemed to become unstable all over again. However, I was twelve. I didn't have a choice.

We crossed San Pablo Avenue and entered the building through a black steel security door. Inside was a small lobby, more like a check-in area, where a staff member sat behind a glass window. It reminded me of the ticket counters at movie theaters, with the speaker slit for conversation. There was no warmth, no sense of permanence here, but I was going to make the best of it.

Up the stairs, down a short hallway, and then we were there. My mom unlocked the door, and I stepped into the space that would be our room. The first thing I noticed was the full-sized bed, centered against the wall, with a nightstand and a small lamp on either side. Against the opposite wall was a TV resting on a small dresser, right next to a window overlooking the bustling street below. It wasn't much, and the carpet, worn and stained, emitted a musty odor that instantly made me feel uncomfortable. But this was where we'd live, and in that moment, being with my mom made it bearable.

Later that day, my dad stopped by after work. He had been staying with his sister, just a short drive away. They were trying to rekindle their relationship while living in separate households, so he came to see me and ended up staying the night. In that tiny, unfamiliar room, for a brief moment, we felt like a family again—a complete family, though not without its fractures. We were together, the three of us, sharing the same space, even if only temporarily. I didn't know it then, but we would only be at the motel for a short time. My mom had found us an apartment just a few blocks away.

We had moved into something new—a chance to start again. But I quickly learned that a change of address doesn't always come with a shift in mindset. Some wounds may heal, but they still remember how to bleed.

CHAPTER 12
New Home, Old Ways

"Let things go! Some things can create stories that shape our inability to preserve what genuinely brings us happiness, leading to a hidden struggle and, ultimately, moments of misery along our journey."

The day finally came when we moved out of the motel and into our new place. It was an old, tri-level apartment painted a faded dark gray, exuding an air of historic charm, though weathered by time. Our unit was on the second floor, and we entered through the back door. Strangely, upon moving in, I noticed we couldn't use the front door. It struck me as odd, perhaps even a fire hazard, but the landlord allowed it, and we didn't know why. Our only entrance was through the back door. After all, rent ran high in California, and landlords often found unconventional ways to accommodate tenants.

Each day, we'd climb the rickety stairs to our apartment, which creaked underfoot but seemed strong enough to support our steps. Inside, the apartment welcomed us with a small kitchen, its fixtures dated but functional. To the right of the kitchen were two bedrooms—mine and my mom's—separated by a narrow bathroom. My room overlooked the street and was modest, just big enough for a bed and a small dresser. Beyond my room lay the living room, a cozy space with built-in wooden cabinets that hinted at the apartment's history. The actual front door, which we couldn't use, was located in the living room—a strange setup, with two doors latched together as if they'd once led to a larger house that had since been divided.

After staying in the apartment for a few weeks, my mom remembered that behind those two locked interior doors in the living room was the original front door of the apartment—the entrance we were prohibited from using. I didn't know if this was the landlord's doing or the neighbor on the other side of the wall who had claimed control, but I knew my mom wouldn't accept it quietly. That wasn't who she was. One day, fed up with having only one way in and out of our place—a risk she couldn't ignore—she decided to test her ability to force her way through. She began to tug and shove at whatever was barricading the door.

It was a heavy wooden bookshelf, tall and thick as if built to withstand a storm. Wedged across the frame, it blocked everything except for a narrow sliver, just enough to reveal a staircase behind it that led to the front door—the one my mom wanted, needed, access to. She gritted her teeth and pushed hard. The wood scraping against the floor echoed like a battle cry through the hallway. The noise was jarring. You could feel it in the walls. It was loud enough to stir someone else.

Suddenly, the door to the other unit swung open. Our neighbor stepped out, yelling and demanding that she stop, insisting she had no right to open that door. It was as if some private arrangement had been made between him and the landlord, some unspoken agreement that gave him claim to that part of the house, that access, and that power. My mom yelled back without flinching. Sweat formed on her brow as her hands still gripped the edge of the shelf. She didn't care about his claims; she cared about our safety—about not being boxed into a place with no escape route. I stood there silently, watching them clash like two forces too tired to explain why life had pushed them to this point.

That was the moment I fully saw him.

On the side of the front door was a narrow windowpane, and through it, I caught a glimpse inside his unit. He must have run out quickly because he was standing in plain view, about 5'11", Hispanic, shoulder-length brown hair that clung to his neck like silk, broad shoulders, a semi-toned frame... and completely naked. Not a thread on him. He stood there as if unbothered by the fact, engaged in a full argument with my mom while revealing every inch of himself to the morning light. My heart jumped. I was stunned—frozen—but not just from shock.

It was the first time I had seen a naked man.

And in that split second, something stirred inside me. A quiet flicker. Not just intrigue, but confusion. Questions I hadn't dared to ask. Feelings I had buried so deep I didn't know they had names. I didn't know if it was attraction, curiosity, or something tangled in the pieces of myself I had long tried to ignore. I just knew that I couldn't look away. Not right away. My gaze lingered until he noticed. His eyes caught mine, and an awkward awareness passed between us. Then, without a word, he turned around and disappeared back inside to put on clothes. Maybe out of embarrassment. Maybe out of decency. Or maybe... because he saw the look in my eyes, too.

Eventually, my mom gave up. Her arms were sore, her voice strained, but her dignity remained intact. She later called the landlord, who confirmed what we had started to suspect. The door couldn't be accessed because he had divided the house into separate units—more tenants meant more money. Safety and fairness weren't part of the business plan.

But that wasn't the only thing divided on that day.

Something inside me split too—a quiet break between who I thought I was and the truths I tried to avoid feeling. I didn't speak. I tucked the moment away. Yet it remained with me, nestled in the folds of memory, resting beside other silences I had yet to find the courage to express aloud.

Not yet.

As I settled into that apartment, I couldn't help but feel a mix of emotions—disappointment, hope, and resilience. I had left behind the familiar comfort of Milwaukee, the closeness of my cousins, and the stability I had found there. However, this was my family, our home, and I was learning to adapt and find meaning in whatever life presented. We had each other, a roof over our heads, and a chance at a fresh start. It wasn't perfect, but for now, it was enough.

* * *

That school year, I was a student at Marcus Foster, a middle school where open lunch was a big deal. Open lunch meant we could go beyond the regular cafeteria food, escape the dull trays of lukewarm offerings, and instead explore a few delicious options outside. I was thrilled, buzzing with anticipation each day for lunch hour. French fries, soda, cookies—simple pleasures, but at that time, they felt like luxury. It was an endless discovery of freedom and indulgence, a break from the ordinary routine, and every bite felt like a taste of something special, something just for me.

I'll never forget the first time I ordered a box of fries. That brown cardboard container with "French Fries" written in a friendly yellow font held pure magic inside. Each fry was golden, crispy on the outside, perfectly salted, and hot. I'd grab a few ketchup packets, carefully squeezing just enough to coat each bite. The combination was a burst of flavor that felt like a tiny rebellion against traditional school lunches. The sense of control—choosing what I wanted, dipping each fry into my little pool of ketchup—was strangely empowering. This freedom to savor each crispy fry or bite into a gooey chocolate chip cookie was heaven for me.

California was like that for me—different from anywhere else I'd been, especially Milwaukee. There was an energy, an open vibe, a feeling that anything was possible. This school had its own pulse. I made a few friends, mostly connections that stayed within school walls. However, there was one friend with whom I clicked. Our bond was built on classes and lunch breaks, an easygoing friendship that felt like a steady presence in my day. He was one of those kids who always had a bit of pocket change, enough to buy himself snacks or drinks, and sometimes, he'd share with me. Growing up in Oakland, I didn't have access to extra money. My mom worked with a fixed income, so I rarely had any cash to call my own. Occasionally, when I stayed with my aunt, she'd slip me a dollar or two, but those instances were few. My friend's generosity meant I could get fries and cookies without worry, allowing me to join in the fun of open lunch.

One day, curious and perhaps a little envious, I asked where he got the money. He shrugged casually and told me his dad gave him money every day. His dad must have been doing well because my friend always had nice clothes—LA Gear sneakers, which were huge at the time, and new outfits. I couldn't relate, as most of my shoes and clothes came secondhand from my cousin. But the cash my friend shared gave me a taste of what it was like to buy things freely, without counting coins or worrying about saving them.

A few days later, I came home with a couple of leftover dollars in my pocket. As I climbed the two flights of stairs to our apartment, I felt the crisp bills in my pocket, proud to have a little spending money. That night, as I was getting ready for bed, my mom saw me with the cash. She asked where I got it, and I told her, "My friend gave it to me." It should've been a simple answer, but her expression changed. Her eyes narrowed, and her face took on a look I'd rarely seen.

"Are you telling me the truth?" she asked, her voice colder than usual.

I nodded, not understanding what she meant. "Yes, Mom. My friend gave it to me at school."

But she didn't believe me.

Her voice rose quickly, sharp like a warning, then spiraled into a storm of accusations. Each word landed with force, not just because of what she said, but because it was her saying it. She looked at me as if I were someone else. Someone slick. Someone who'd trade his character for quick cash. She accused me of running drugs, of lying, of hiding things from her. I stood there, stunned, the money I had in my pocket suddenly feeling like evidence. I tried to explain—again and again—that a friend had helped me. But she wasn't hearing me. She had already made up her mind.

She wasn't seeing the boy in front of her. She was seeing ghosts—memories of men who'd failed her, moments of survival she'd had to claw through alone. Her fear had turned me into a suspect. The verdict had already been reached, and I hadn't even finished my sentence.

It broke something in me.

I had worked hard to stay out of trouble, make good decisions, and avoid being one more thing she had to worry about. I had grown up faster than most kids my age, forced by life to carry burdens in silence—responsibility, disappointment, even her pain. I had done everything possible to remain steady in our chaos. But none of that mattered now. Not to her. Not in that moment.

It serves as a reminder of the same kind of irrational rage I experienced in the past, present now, not rooted in fact but in fear. And fear, when it festers, distorts everything. I knew her anger wasn't really about me; it was about all the things she couldn't control and all the ways life had hurt her. But knowing that didn't make it easier to stand there and be accused. It didn't lessen the sting of betrayal.

I felt a quiet shame wash over me, as if I had done something wrong simply by being helped by someone else, just by receiving something she hadn't given. I wanted to shout, cry, and ask her why she couldn't *see* me. But I didn't. I swallowed it down, like I always did.

What I needed in that moment wasn't suspicion—it was grace. A little trust. A little recognition of the boy I was trying so hard to become. But instead, I stood in front of my own mother, bearing the weight of being misunderstood by the one person I had spent my whole life trying to protect.

That night, she continued to yell and question me. "Where did you get the money, Keyimani?" she demanded. "Tell me the truth!" I was telling the truth, but she wasn't ready to hear it. Finally, she told me we would go to school together the next day to get to the bottom of things. Her suspicions hadn't faded, and she was determined to prove them. She wanted to confront the principal, the teachers, whoever she needed to, so she could "find out what was really going on."

The next morning, I went to school with her, feeling uneasy and embarrassed. We went straight to the office, where she explained to the principal that I had been coming home with money and that she suspected something shady. I knew my friend would be called in soon, and I started to feel guilty for dragging him into my mom's suspicions.

NEW HOME, OLD WAYS

The principal had my friend come to the office, and there he was, confused and nervous. They asked him about the money, and he explained it was from his dad. But just when I thought that would be enough, the principal called his dad for confirmation. His dad was honest—he admitted giving his son money but said it wasn't every day, and even he sounded uncertain now. My friend's face fell, and I realized that my mom's accusations had started a ripple effect that none of us could escape.

When school ended that day, I was left with a feeling of dread, wondering if my friend's dad would scold him the same way my mom had scolded me.

The next day, when I saw my friend by his locker, I felt both relieved and anxious to know how things had gone. He told me that when he got home, his dad confronted him about the money, eventually discovering that he'd been taking small amounts of loose dollars and coins from a stash. His dad was upset, but my friend assured him he'd stop.

Although the truth had emerged, my mom still wasn't convinced. The whole ordeal left a sour taste, as though my innocence had been permanently tainted. She continued to believe I was hiding something, clinging to her suspicions about drugs. Her lack of trust hurt, and I could feel the bond between us fraying. In her mind, I was guilty of something I hadn't done, and it was a shadow I couldn't escape. In the end, her suspicions drove her to make a final decision: I'd leave California. This time, I wouldn't come back.

Looking back, it felt like a sad twist of fate. My friend's kindness, my first taste of freedom and choice, had turned into something dark and twisted. I would leave behind California, Marcus Foster, and the open lunches that had brought me such simple happiness. The memory of those golden fries and those carefree moments would stay with me, a bittersweet reminder of the innocence I lost too soon.

New walls couldn't hide the echoes of old wounds—and deep down, I knew healing couldn't be packed into a moving box.

CHAPTER 13
Rebuilding Roots

"Stability is essential—it gives us something to look forward to, a routine, a promise, and a foundation of trust. It's even more fulfilling when built with someone you love and who loves you in return."

Returning to Milwaukee was like slipping into a version of life I'd nearly forgotten. So much had changed—friends had moved on, routines had shifted, and my aunt had started over in a new neighborhood. But some things remained, like how her house, even in transition, felt like a refuge.

Aunt Grace had moved to a quieter part of town. The rumble of distant trains became part of the soundtrack of my adolescence. Her duplex served as our headquarters for healing. It wasn't fancy but faithful—steady in a way I didn't know I needed.

When I enrolled at Edison Middle School, I walked streets that didn't ask me to shrink or perform. I found friends and freedom in little things—like crossing railroad tracks, daring myself to feel brave again. Slowly, I started anchoring myself, not because life stopped shifting, but because I had begun to find rhythm within the shifts.

It was the first time I wondered—maybe home wasn't a place where nothing changed. Perhaps it was a place that allowed you to change and still remain whole.

My aunt moved not only for us but also for my grandmother, who was eager to leave Chicago and be closer to her daughter. Ours was a mixed household by blood but solid by bond. My aunt was not related to me by blood but by marriage; she and my other aunts and uncles shared the same father but had different mothers. In our family, we didn't use titles like "stepsister" or "half-cousin." You were family, and that meant you were treated as such. Aunt Grace had a big-hearted way of opening her life to those around her, and I was no exception. She loved us unconditionally, offering her time, attention, and home as fully as any mother would.

In this new house, though, I had to make new adjustments. First up was finding a school. It was the middle of the school year by the time I returned, and there was no guarantee I could find a place that late. But, as always, my family found a way to make it work. I had a cousin who lived down the street from Edison Middle School, and that connection opened the door for me to enroll in the second semester. Edison was close enough to walk—just a couple of miles down quiet, tree-lined streets that seemed worlds away from the noisy, packed streets of California. It was a fresh start, a blank slate.

When school started, I fell in with a group of friends who were always up for an adventure. We discovered a shortcut along the railroad tracks that kept us off the main streets and offered a little taste of danger to start and end each day. These weren't just any tracks; they ran above a creek with a twenty-foot drop, leaving only a thin rail between us and the edge. And then there were the trains—long, cargo-laden giants cutting through the city with horns that could be heard for miles. We'd have to dash off the tracks to avoid them sometimes, our hearts racing, feeling both the thrill and fear of that narrow escape. Occasionally, I'd take my younger cousins on that same shortcut, showing them the ropes, and I could see the mix of terror and excitement in their faces. If a train's horn blasted while we were on the tracks, we'd take off at a sprint, not daring to look back.

Edison became a community for me. Some teachers had a genuine interest in their students' lives. Not all of them, of course, but those who did significantly impacted me. From music to social studies to science, they were a consistent presence. They encouraged my curiosity, supported my goals, and uplifted me in ways I needed more than I had realized. At Edison, I took up the alto saxophone—my first instrument. I initially wanted to play the trumpet, but since I joined the band mid-year, they handed me the sax instead. It was just as rewarding, and I spent hours learning how to coax music from its brass body.

One of my favorite memories from Edison was our eighth-grade camping trip. We left the classroom behind for nearly a week and headed to a campsite where we cooked our meals, learned outdoor skills, and spent entire days fishing—a skill I had perfected over the summers with my aunt. I showed off a little, catching fish faster than the others, and it felt good to share what I knew. That trip was special, offering a taste of freedom and a glimpse of the world outside the city. Camping, cooking, and learning together—these were experiences I might never have had if I had stayed in California.

I looked forward to high school when middle school ended, but it marked a bittersweet milestone. My relationship with my mom had grown more distant since I left California. Whether it was due to the challenges of her own life or some hidden resentment, we barely spoke, and by eighth grade, our connection was nearly nonexistent. I went through the rest of middle school without her by my side, and when I graduated, neither of my parents was there to cheer me on. It was a happy day, surrounded by friends and teachers who cared; yet, there lingered a shadow—a longing for their presence, for that feeling of being embraced by my family's love.

Graduation came and went, and even though I was surrounded by people who cared deeply about me, there was a unique ache in missing my parents' presence. Every kid, especially a little Black boy, longs for that. That love, that connection, is like an anchor, grounding you as you step into the next phase of life.

I didn't know it then, but that distance wasn't just physical—it was the beginning of something I'd carry for years. Being away from her felt, in many ways, like losing her. Not to death, but to silence. To space. To unspoken disappointment and unresolved pain. She wasn't there, and eventually, I stopped expecting her to be. That kind of absence seeps in quietly, like a slow leak in the foundation, and before you know it, you're standing in the ruins of something that used to feel whole.

I had learned to keep moving, achieving, and smiling even when my heart had questions it was too afraid to ask. Why didn't she call? Why didn't she write? Did she still see me as her son? Did she love me the same? But I buried those questions behind the walls I had started building around myself. In doing so, I began to shape how I would handle absence for the rest of my life.

When people left, I didn't cry. I adjusted. When someone passed away, I stayed strong—for others, for myself, for the little boy who had learned early that even when someone is still alive, you can still feel the ache of losing them. The slow unraveling of that maternal bond taught me that not all loss is loud; some of it is quiet, a fading voice on the other end of the line, a birthday missed, a graduation seat left empty.

In the spaces where cement met soul, I started to rebuild not just my room—but a version of me that could grow beyond the rubble. But even in that pain, I pressed forward. I kept showing up. That's the thing about resilience—sometimes it isn't loud or celebrated. Sometimes it's just the quiet act of rising again, believing in your worth, even when those who helped shape you forget to remind you.

CHAPTER 14
Breaking the Cycle

"Options are choices that demand careful consideration of future consequences. Each one calls for the wisdom to think long-term, as a single wrong decision can delay the destiny God has designed for you."

I was always told, "Go to school, get a good education." The words echoed throughout my childhood—a mantra from my mother I clung to, even if I didn't fully understand why. Growing up, my mom had her way of instilling discipline in me, demanding nothing short of good grades. Her no-nonsense approach meant that anything less than a B grade was unacceptable. Failing to meet her expectations often ended in the ritual of "picking three switches"—a harsh reality of discipline that I dreaded. It wasn't out of cruelty, but rather out of fear for my future, a fear that I didn't yet share but would one day come to appreciate.

When I lived in Oakland, if I got into trouble, it wouldn't take long for my mom to find out and set me straight. I remember one day in elementary school, back at Bella Vista, when I was in trouble. I can't recall the exact reason—a stray piece of paper thrown at the wrong moment, or maybe talking out of turn. Whatever it was, it landed me in detention, which meant I'd be home late. I knew I'd have to answer for it. Coming home later than usual required an explanation, and none I could give would keep me out of trouble.

Walking the familiar five or six blocks home felt like a slow march to judgment day. In California, some blocks are unusually long—stretching like three blocks rolled into one. The last block was always the hardest, though. A long hill dipped down before rising again, leading up to a vantage point where you could see most of the neighborhood sprawled out below. My friend Walter's house was right at the top, and from that spot, my mom had a clear view down to the main road, where I'd eventually appear walking home. Today, she was waiting by the window, watching.

I crossed the busy street, feeling the weight of what awaited me. The front door creaked open, and she stood at the top of the stairs with a belt clenched tightly in her hand. Her face was hard, and I could sense her fury before she spoke. "Why are you just now getting home?" Her voice was sharp, edged with concern and anger that I hadn't anticipated. When I replied that I had detention, her frustration boiled over, and suddenly she was coming down the stairs with a force that made me backpedal. She wanted to take me back to school as if to confront the teacher holding me back. I don't know if she thought I was lying or wanted answers, but her determination terrified me.

We started the journey back, a silent march through the neighborhood where everyone seemed to be outside, enjoying the evening sun. The building next to ours housed a few friends, and James, one of my closest friends, lived nearby. I could feel their eyes on us as we crossed 14th Avenue, the street I crossed every morning, but now charged with tension. And then, without warning, she stopped, yanked me back, and began to swing the belt. Right there on the street, she unleashed her frustration, yelling and striking me as the neighbors and my friends watched.

Shame and confusion flooded me. As I looked around and saw the familiar faces of my friends, the words spilled out of me, "I hate you!" Then, I ran. I ran, my feet pounding the pavement as tears stung my eyes. I couldn't understand why it had come to this. Why would she do this to me in front of everyone? I was hurt, humiliated, and confused. Did I deserve this? Was I such a bad kid? These questions echoed in my mind as I finally stopped, breathless, on a small hill where I could still see the back of our apartment building. The sun began to set, casting long shadows across the neighborhood, and slowly, the weight of my actions began to settle in. I knew I couldn't stay away forever.

When I walked back, the twilight had deepened, and my mom stood by a police car in front of our building. She looked hurt, clutching the belt and talking to the officer. I realized then that my words had cut her deeply. She wasn't just angry—she was hurt, maybe even heartbroken, by my rejection. The officer asked me if I wanted to stay or if I'd prefer to go somewhere else, and I chose to go live with my aunt in Berkeley for a while. That marked the start of something I wouldn't fully grasp until much later—a realization that the pain of that day, as much as it stung, was a force that pushed me to seek a different path.

* * *

Later, I lived in Milwaukee with my Aunt Grace and three cousins. Aunt Grace took on the role of caregiver for her grandchildren, aiming to keep the family together and on track, a duty she held with fierce determination. We were a typical Black family, close-knit and bound by a sense of resilience. Our time together brought warmth I hadn't felt back in Oakland. My grandmother lived upstairs, having moved from Chicago, while my cousin and I shared rooms in the basement. Privacy was scarce, with walls made of old plywood, but it was enough for us. The foundation would leak on rainy days, allowing water to seep into the basement. The water would soak the carpet, leaving a damp, musty scent. Yet, we didn't mind; we were content with the little space we had to call our own.

I grew close to my oldest cousin, who embodied confidence and charisma. She was what people call now, "thick," around 5'1", with caramel skin and dimples that could make anyone melt. She knew the effect she had on others and wore it like armor. On warm summer nights and lazy weekends, we'd find ourselves in the dim glow of the kitchen, well past midnight, laughing and talking quietly so as not to wake the others. The scent of peanut butter filled the air as we measured flour, sugar, and that smooth, golden spread. My cousin had this way of mixing the dough, her hands nimble and practiced, moving with the care of someone who knew their way around a kitchen. She was a natural—a little bit of flour smudged on her cheek, her hair pulled back, eyes intent on getting the cookies just right. She had a knack for turning the simplest ingredients into something that felt like a treat meant just for us. The oven hummed softly, its warm light casting shadows as the dough rose, filling the house with a smell so sweet and comforting that it made the late hour the perfect time to bake.

While we waited for the cookies to bake, she began to talk, her voice dropping as she shared stories of her dating escapades. She leaned against the table, a mischievous smile playing on her lips as she described her latest encounters—the guys she met, the funny mishaps, and unexpected turns in her adventures. I was younger and looked up to her with awe and curiosity, laughing at her witty remarks and absorbing her tales of romance and drama like a distant saga. Her stories were equally thrilling and hilarious, full of moments that made me see her in a new light—this bold and beautiful cousin who captured the attention of everyone she met. I caught a glimpse of life beyond my years; her stories were a preview of the world waiting beyond our own. Those nights became a memory I carried with me—a blend of laughter, secrets, and the rich, familiar taste of cookies shared in the stillness of the night.

Then there was Jamal, my cousin, who felt more like a brother. He was tall, with skin in the deep shade of polished mahogany, and had a body chiseled by hours spent on the basketball court and doing push-ups in the basement. Jamal carried a swagger, a quiet confidence that didn't need to be announced. It was clear to anyone who crossed his path that he was a force, a figure who commanded respect just by being there. The neighborhood knew him not only for his looks but for his reputation—a no-nonsense guy who didn't seek trouble but certainly wouldn't back down from it. He possessed street wisdom that couldn't be taught; everyone knew better than to test him. He was a natural leader in our world, the kind of person people deferred to with a nod or a look, an unspoken acknowledgment of his presence.

Jamal was a ladies' man who could charm anyone with a smirk or a few well-chosen words. The girls flocked to him, drawn by the aura of mystery he wore so well. He moved through life as if he had a map no one else could see, and honestly, I admired him for it. He had a way of being bold without needing to say much—a rare combination of charisma and grit.

Though we were cousins, we were as close as brothers. We were inseparable, bound by family and friendship, and fought like brothers. Our fights resulted in bruises and scrapes, small battles in our childhood wars, each strengthening our bond. Jamal constantly pushed me, ensuring I knew how to hold my own, teaching me with his fists and sharp words that life wouldn't be easy. But it was never out of malice; it was his way of showing love, of passing down a toughness he knew I'd need. He was like my drill sergeant, starting personal fights and daring me to back down, only to laugh and throw his arm around me when it was all over. He didn't have a little brother, so I filled that role—one I took on proudly.

We didn't need to say we loved each other; it was evident in every punch, shared secret, and late-night talk on the house's back steps when the streetlights buzzed overhead. I knew he'd have my back in any situation, just as I'd have his, and that trust was rare and precious. Our fights, our shared laughter, and the bond we built taught me strength, loyalty, and a kind of love that didn't need words. Even in those rough moments, I knew he was looking out for me, shaping me in his way.

Then there was Phylicia, the youngest among us. She was the sweetest of us all, but also a force of her own—a real tomboy with a fierce competitive streak. While most girls in the neighborhood might've been caught playing Double Dutch or hanging out on the porch, you'd find her in the alley alongside us, running plays and dribbling like she was born with a basketball. Her energy was infectious, and her laughter had a way of lightening even the most intense moments of our games. She could run, jump, and throw elbows like any of us; half the time, she'd leave the boys trailing in her dust.

Our "court" was nothing fancy. It was our makeshift kingdom: a milk crate with the bottom cut out and nailed high on a wooden post, just the right height to make it feel official, at least to us. That crate endured its fair share of beatings over the years but held strong, becoming the heartbeat of our games, meets, and rivalries. The alley was dusty, with cracked asphalt and loose gravel underfoot, but it was where we all came alive. We'd spend hours out there, the sun dipping lower and lower in the sky as we played, oblivious to the world outside our game.

And there she was, right in the thick of it—chasing down loose balls, juking us with moves she picked up from watching the guys play, calling out scores, and taunting like a pro. She never wanted special treatment just because she was the only girl there. She was our equal and sometimes our fiercest opponent.

The neighborhood kids would also gather around, forming teams that sometimes became full-fledged tournaments. She was natural, able to hold her own against the best of us, and always strived to prove she was just as strong and skilled. There was something beautiful in the way she played; a raw joy and freedom, as if the whole world faded away when she had that ball. She was a girl, yes, but also a kind of legend in her own right, showing us all that strength could come in surprising forms, even from someone with such a kind, sweet spirit.

* * *

We all attended Rufus King High School except for my oldest cousin, who attended a different school. My cousins and I walked to school together, and each morning, Aunt Grace would call out from the top of the stairs, her voice a morning bell that pulled us from sleep. "Y'all get up, it's time for school! Do y'all hear me?" We'd reply, "Yes, ma'am," a call-and-response that cemented our respect for her and her sacrifices. But life didn't go as planned. Over time, Jamal's dedication to school started to wane. He had grown tired of the routine, convinced that the daily grind wasn't for him anymore. It was as if he had been planning it for a while, letting go bit by bit, until the final decision felt inevitable. One morning, after my aunt's usual call from the top of the stairs, there was no response from his room. My cousin had made up his mind; he was done with school. It was hard to believe as I watched him walk out that door, knowing he'd decided to leave his education behind. By his junior year, he was out, leaving a hole in the household that neither Phylicia nor I could ignore.

Phylicia and I kept going, though we were the last two standing—the only ones left upholding my aunt's constant reminder: "Get an education." She believed it with every fiber of her being—that this path could shape our futures, no matter how tough or unglamorous it seemed some days. She said it repeatedly, as if speaking it enough would make us believe it even more deeply, as if it could root itself in us like the foundation of a house.

By my junior year, I was beginning to discover my own rhythm, and it was through music. I had developed a bit of a reputation at school for my singing. I'd joined the concert and the gospel choir, places that felt like they were made for me. During science class, whenever we had a little free time, a small group of us would gather at the back of the room, and we'd sing. I remember those afternoons well; we'd harmonize to whatever was popular then, and I'd strive to reach that perfect high note that would give the girls goosebumps. Songs like Sadie by R. Kelly and If I Ever Fall in Love by Shai were our go-to tracks, with a timeless kind of soul, the sort of music you could get lost in. And when I hit those high notes just right, I'd see the look on the girls' faces, a mix of wonder and awe. I'd forget everything else briefly, even the struggles at home.

* * *

But that sense of steady purpose was short-lived. We had finished the first semester and were at the tail end of our Christmas break when Phylicia decided she wouldn't return. She didn't want to finish her senior year; she chose to step away for her own reasons, just as her sister and brother had. I could barely take it in. Another cousin was gone; another person lost to a path I was beginning to fear was inevitable.

It hurt. There I was, alone again—the last one still striving to meet my aunt's hope, to the promise she had drilled into us: stay in school, build something for yourself. But now, that promise felt like a weight, heavy and isolating. They were all gone. One by one, my cousins had dropped out, slipping through the cracks Aunt Grace had spent her life trying to seal shut. And with each one who walked away, I felt a deeper pressure to stay. To succeed. To hold the line.

Because the truth was that I didn't feel I had a choice.

Dropping out would have felt like a betrayal. Aunt Grace had taken me in, fed me when I didn't have food, kept the lights on when my world went dark, and offered me something more valuable than anything I could hold—stability. She never said it outright, but I could see it in her eyes when another one left school. The way her smile would tighten. She'd sigh a little longer than usual as she stirred her coffee. That kind of sadness didn't need words. It was in how she carried herself—strong on the outside, but chipped in places we didn't know how to fix.

She didn't have to say it because I already knew: her heart broke every time one of us gave up on the very thing she sacrificed to protect—our future. She had worked so hard to keep us together, to give us something resembling a family. And walking away from school, from that opportunity, from her vision? That would've been like slapping her in the face.

I couldn't do it.

Not because I was stronger or better, but because I owed her more than that. I also owed myself more than that. The cycle stopped with me; it had to.

And if I'm honest, there was something else driving me, too—something less noble but just as powerful. I needed leverage. I needed to be able to look my parents in the face one day and let them know that this—this diploma, this milestone, this man I was becoming—wasn't because of them. It wasn't born of their guidance or their presence. They hadn't seen the late nights, the pain, and the moments when I wanted to give up and didn't. This wasn't their victory; it was mine. And Aunt Grace's.

I wanted to prove something—to the world, to myself. That my circumstances didn't get the final say in who I'd become. That the cards I'd been dealt, ragged and torn at the edges, could still win the game if I played them right. That's why I stayed. That's why I kept going. Because I had something to prove—and someone to honor.

So no, finishing high school wasn't optional; it was my protest, my promise, my quiet rebellion against everything that tried to count me out.

Graduation arrived, bringing with it a bittersweet sense of accomplishment. I stood alone, a testament to my aunt's sacrifices and my mother's insistence on education. I felt proud, knowing I had broken a cycle and carved a path forward. Yet as I accepted my diploma, a hollow feeling crept in. Neither of my parents was there to witness this moment. I knew my mom was still in California, but she hadn't made the trip, and my dad was little more than a ghost, rumored to be wandering the streets of Berkeley or at San Pablo Park. Their absence lingered, casting a shadow over the triumph.

But even in that void, I knew one thing: their absence had, in its own way, pushed me to become more. Through every hardship, I found strength, and with every difficult memory, I built a resilience that would carry me forward. In that moment, I realized the answer to the question that had haunted me since childhood: why education mattered. It was my way out, my way forward, a key to a life beyond the hardships I'd endured, and a hope that my journey might one day inspire others to break free, too.

There comes a time when you can no longer outrun the past. No matter how many new addresses you write down or how many new versions of yourself you try to create, the old wounds find their way back. They find you in the stillness—in the quiet moments when no one else is around to distract you.

Healing doesn't begin with movement; it begins with standing still. It involves daring to look in the mirror and seeing not just who you have survived to become, but also the scars you have picked up along the way.

This is the space between who you were and who you are about to choose to be—the place where cycles either continue or finally break.

MIRRORS AND CROSSROADS

*"This is the space between who you were and
who you are about to choose to be."*

At some point, you have to stop running and look in the mirror. What you see might scare you. It might confuse you. It might demand something you've never given yourself: honesty.

These are the chapters where I faced regret, held love I didn't know how to embrace and made decisions I couldn't undo. Here, grace didn't feel like a soft blanket—it felt like a knife piercing my skin. Pain, real and sharp, became the teacher I couldn't escape. The past knocked louder, and the consequences landed harder.

And still, I was choosing. I was choosing whether to continue the cycle or become the disruption, whether to carry bitterness or to birth healing, whether to become the man I feared or the one I needed.

This is where mirrors were no longer just reflections. They became reckonings and crossroads that offered a space for transformation to become possible—but only if I was willing to be changed.

CHAPTER 15
The Weight of Regret

"Days are gifts, second chances granted by God, offering us the opportunity to begin anew. As individuals, we must extend that same grace to others—a grace that rises above past mistakes, disappointment, and hurt. Extend that same grace."

People always say you shouldn't live life with regrets, that you should move forward and let the past rest where it belongs. But that's not how it is for me. I have one regret that I can't shake, one memory that lingers, a single decision that haunts me with the question of "what if?" Her name was Ariana. She caught your attention when she entered a room—with a magnetic charm that made everything feel lighter. Her hair flowed in soft waves, her mocha skin glowed, and her smile lit up the space around her. When she looked at me, my heart raced. But it wasn't just her looks—how she laughed, moved, and made me feel like I was walking on air. From the moment we met, I fell a little more each time our paths crossed.

Throughout most of high school, we had a slow-burning chemistry that never quite ignited. We'd flirt and hang out in the same circles, and for a while, it seemed like we were on the verge of something, only to be held back by timing or circumstances. Finally, senior year rolled around, and for the first time, everything fell into place. I had just come out of a relationship after being dumped in junior year, and I was starting my senior year single. I was finally free. So was Ariana. We began seeing each other in a way that wasn't just passing glances or playful smiles; it was real. We started dating, and for the first time, I felt like I was exactly where I was supposed to be.

* * *

Prom night was a turning point. I remember every detail as if it happened yesterday. I pulled up to Ariana's house in my pastor's 1989 burgundy Lincoln Continental, a car he had trusted me with for the evening. I had worked hard for that moment, serving in the church from the age of fourteen, and my pastor had become something of a mentor and father figure to me. The car gleamed, freshly detailed, and the leather interior was pristine. I felt like a king, pulling up to Ariana's house with that corsage in my hand, ready to take her to the highlight of our senior year.

Alford, K. (1998). *Freshman Year* [Photograph]. Milwaukee, Wisconsin: Keywords Unlocked, LLC

THE WEIGHT OF REGRET

I knocked on her door, and her parents greeted me with smiles and open arms, inviting me in as they had done a hundred times before. "She's almost ready," they said. I waited in the living room, trying to keep my cool while exchanging small talk with her parents, assuring them that I'd keep her safe that night. And then Ariana walked in. The moment I saw her, my breath caught. She was stunning—more beautiful than I could have imagined. She glided around the corner in a dress that seemed made for her, her hair cascading around her shoulders. I slipped the corsage onto her wrist, feeling the thrill of her touch, and for that one moment, everything felt perfect. We left the house heading to the prom, where we danced the night away, completely lost in each other, and for the first time, I knew that this was the beginning of something special.

After prom, Ariana and I became inseparable. We were high school sweethearts, our hearts set on the future, our dreams interwoven. We had plans—we were going to the same college, ready to take on life together. The first semester began, and while Ariana moved into the dorms to soak up the full college experience, I stayed at home, commuting to campus each day. Still, we found time to be together.

* * *

Whenever I was free between classes or shifts at Hardee's, where I'd been working since I was fourteen, I'd find her, and we'd make the most of every moment. We'd double date with friends, explore the campus, and fall deeper into the thrill of young love. But college brought freedom and change, and with that came the unexpected. Ariana immersed herself in campus life, made new friends, attended parties, and engaged in all the experiences that came with college. And me? I was working long hours, juggling school and my job, trying to keep up with my responsibilities while she lived the life I'd only glimpsed from the outside. This created a distance between us, one that I hadn't realized was growing until it was too late.

* * *

However, sometimes life shakes you, not to break you, but to sober you up. It reminds you how close you are to something that could change your world forever. That day, I was on campus like any other, caught in the routine of classes and spending hours after being at Hardee's, trying to balance the weight of becoming a man before I even knew what manhood required of me. Then my phone rang. It was Ariana.

Her voice was unusually quiet. "Can you come by?" she said. "We need to talk."

I paused. My first thought was—did her meal plan run out again? Did she need help getting food from the cafeteria in her dorm, or maybe she just didn't want to stay there anymore? We had grown close—closer than either of us had probably expected. We had shared moments that many college students do, where the line between love and exploration is blurred by the thrill of freedom and the depth of intimacy. But what she needed to say that day… I wasn't ready for it. I should've been because of our actions and decisions, but I wasn't.

I walked to her dorm, my mind racing through a list of possibilities, none of which prepared me for what I was about to hear. She opened the door slowly. Her face was blank yet pale, as if she'd rehearsed a hundred ways to begin and still came up empty. I kissed her lightly and made my way to the chair beside her bed—the chair that had practically become mine over the past few months.

She stood in front of me, shifting her weight from one foot to the other. Then, with a heavy breath, she said it. "My period hasn't come," she whispered. "I think I might be pregnant."

Time paused, and it felt like my heart dropped out of my chest. All I could say in that moment of sheer, unfiltered emotion was, "Oh shit."

Not out of joy. Not out of anger. Just fear. Raw and paralyzing. Fear of what this meant. What would people think? What would our families say? What would happen to us, two kids who had only just begun to step into the world on our own? We were 19—just freshmen—still figuring out how to study for exams and navigate financial aid forms, and now we were confronting the reality of potentially becoming parents?

Yeah, this scared me completely. I wanted to disappear from that room while also wanting to protect it, her, and us.

But something inside me shifted. I looked up and saw her tears beginning to form—full of the same uncertainty, the same fear, the same questions I was facing—and I knew I couldn't leave her alone in it.

THE WEIGHT OF REGRET

"Okay," I said slowly, reaching for her hand. "We'll think through this together. We'll confirm first, but if it's real… I'm not going anywhere."

I kissed her gently on the forehead, and in that moment, I meant every word. We were both scared. And truthfully, I wasn't sure what would come next. But I knew enough to understand this wasn't the time to run. It was the time to stay. To stand with her and for us.

I didn't know then that this night—this vulnerable, confusing, terrifying moment—would be the foundation for an even greater storm. I didn't know that days later, she would reveal a truth that would rip through that promise we made to each other like paper in the wind. That same fear she felt, the confusion she carried, was tied to more than just a missed period. It was tied to something she had done. Something I wasn't prepared to hear.

But before that, in that dorm room, in that chair next to her bed, I believed we could face anything.

I believed we were in this together.

* * *

Time had passed since the pregnancy scare, and we went on with our lives as if everything were normal—attending classes, spending time together, and hanging out with friends on a few local trips around the city. Back then, I drove a Ford Taurus in an odd shade of green. It was one of the first cars I'd ever gotten from a dealership, and I was proud of it. That car gave Ariana and me the freedom to go on dates whenever we weren't working, in class, or buried in our studies.

One afternoon, Ariana called me—her voice carrying that same uneasy quiet it had the last time she needed to tell me something serious. It stopped me in my tracks. I knew that tone: it was soft, careful… almost afraid. My heart dropped, and my mind raced, just like before.

By the time I reached her dorm, my chest was tight with nerves. Oh God, I thought, is she about to tell me she's *actually* pregnant this time? The thought looped over and over as I ascended the stairs.

She opened the door slowly. Her eyes met mine, and I could see it—she was just as nervous as I was, maybe even more. Her hands trembled slightly as she stepped aside to let me in. I walked over to the chair near the window— the same spot I always sat in—but it didn't feel familiar this time. It felt like a waiting room before a storm.

I sat down and looked at her. She was pacing, trying to find the right words. Then, without much warning, she stopped and said it.

She told me the truth.

And that truth... shattered everything.

There had been a party over the weekend, there had been alcohol, and at that moment, she had gotten too drunk to think straight. She had ended up in bed with another guy, an athlete on campus—a basketball player. I sat there dazed, as I couldn't believe what I was hearing. The girl I had loved for years, the girl I had waited for, had betrayed me. She stood there, tears streaming down her face, apologizing, saying it meant nothing and that she had been too drunk to understand. But the damage was done. I walked out, numb with betrayal.

* * *

For weeks, I kept my distance, pushing her away and refusing to let her make amends. She tried again and again, even coming over one night to talk while I was cooking. She sat on the floor, pleading and apologizing, and I could see how much she wanted to make things right. But I couldn't bring myself to forgive her. I was too hurt, too angry, and too caught up in my pain to see past it. I didn't see her as the girl I had loved for years; I saw her as someone who had broken my trust, and in my mind, I couldn't get past it.

Eventually, she gave up. She left, tears in her eyes, running to her car and driving away. I watched her go, telling myself it was for the best. She had hurt me, and I couldn't bear to let her do it again. But as the years passed, I realized how wrong I had been. Ariana had been my friend, my love, and I had let her slip away because of a forgivable mistake that I now see as something I should have let go of.

Time passed, and I moved forward, but Ariana never truly left my thoughts. Years later, I learned that she had become pregnant by an old boyfriend and had moved out of town. Then, one day, I received the news: Ariana was gone, taken from this world in a violent argument, her life ended by someone who had no regard for the light she carried. When I heard this, I felt like I'd lost her all over again. And this time, there was no chance to make things right, no way to take back the hurtful words, the cold silence, the times I'd turned her away when all she wanted was forgiveness.

* * *

I often think of Ariana, wondering how things could have been different. If only I had let go of my pride, had forgiven her, or had held onto her when she needed me most—maybe our paths would have changed. Now, I live with the weight of that regret, a constant reminder that everyone deserves a second chance. Forgiveness isn't just about letting someone back into your life; it's a gift we give ourselves. Ariana taught me this, even if her absence was the price I paid to understand it.

Looking back, I see now that I didn't fully understand what grace really meant—not until I lost someone I cared deeply about. I used to think that being strong meant cutting people off when they hurt you, and that if someone let you down, it was smarter to walk away before they could do it again. But the truth is, I was just scared: scared of being disappointed again, scared of giving someone the chance to hurt me the way my dad once did.

When someone breaks a promise to you—especially someone close to you—it lingers. It makes it harder to trust and more difficult to offer second chances. I carried that pain with me, often without even realizing it. When Ariana and I faced problems, I didn't react solely to her actions. I responded to all the hurt I had ever bottled up inside. I shut her out, not because I didn't care, but because I cared too deeply and didn't know how to cope with that fear.

Giving second chances isn't easy. It means forgiving when it's hard, believing that people can change, and sometimes staying when everything inside you says to run. With Ariana, I didn't fight for us as I should have; I let fear take over. I carry that as one of the hardest lessons I've ever learned.

When someone matters to you—really matters—you don't simply walk away. You stay. You fight. You show up repeatedly until there's truly nothing left to give. But I gave up too soon. Not because I didn't love her, but because I didn't know how to love her while still carrying my own pain.

Now I understand that offering grace doesn't mean forgetting what happened. It means seeing the person for who they are—and who they're

OAKLAND HILLS, MILWAUKEE RIVERS

trying to become. I think about that a lot—about what could've happened if I'd tried a little harder and how grace might have saved what fear destroyed.

So now, when I'm given the chance to show grace, I take it. I know what it feels like to lose something that still had life left in it. I experienced the weight of regret and never want to carry that kind of silence again.

CHAPTER 16
Unspoken Expectations

"Sometimes, habits create barriers to overcoming disappointment and hurt. These habits, if not addressed, have the potential to destroy things you've fought so hard to repair."

The day my mother visited felt like a culmination of so many emotions—years of separation, forgiveness, and the quiet, persistent hope that we could mend what had been untended for so long. I had imagined her arrival so many times, almost like a scene from a movie: the airport, the happy reunion, and her sharing in one of the biggest achievements of my life. I'd worked hard to get here, to make something of myself, and I wanted her to see it. The idea of her coming to Milwaukee to witness my graduation with my master's degree was something I clung to, a symbol of healing and the start of something new.

The day had finally arrived. Her flight was scheduled to land in Chicago, and I drove the hour down from Milwaukee, nervous as I made my way to the airport. After finding her again, I went to California as often as possible, hoping each visit would help make up for the time we had lost. Rebuilding our relationship was something I cherished. Even when it was hard, I saw it as a path toward forgiving her—and, in a way, forgiving myself for the feelings of abandonment I had carried. This was different, though. It felt like she was coming into my world this time, on my terms, to see who I had become.

At baggage claim, I spotted her standing near the carousel, her head turned as if she were already scanning for me. She seemed smaller than I remembered, and I hurried to her with a wide smile, ready to embrace her. We hugged, and the weight of years melted away a little in her arms. Then, I noticed the suitcase—a colossal thing, the kind someone packs for a long trip or even a permanent move.

We made our way to the car, lugging the suitcase. I attributed it to her being cautious or just wanting enough clothes for the rest of the summer. After all, this was California to Wisconsin. But as we hit the highway back to Milwaukee, she finally said what I couldn't have predicted in a thousand years. She looked at me and said, "I'm staying here in Milwaukee with you!"

I could feel the shock spread across my face. I looked over at her, mouth open, searching her face for some hint that she was joking. "Wait… you're staying? With whom?" I finally asked. She looked back at me with a soft smile and said, "With you." The words hung between us like a flare in the dark. I took a breath, realizing this wasn't just a visit to attend my graduation. This was a move she had kept to herself until now, and she expected me to shift everything to make it work. I swallowed as my mind raced with thoughts.

I wasn't prepared for this. I wasn't expecting to suddenly have a housemate, especially my mother, whose presence in my life had always been a mix of love and old wounds. I tried to steady my voice, carefully explaining, "Mom, I have a roommate. I can't just have you move in. We set everything up so you could stay with Big Momma, remember? That was the plan." Her face fell, her expression shifting from surprise to something deeper, something wounded. She had counted on me and expected that I would be ready to welcome her without hesitation, to let her stay even without the slightest warning. She hadn't said anything about moving or asked if it would be okay—she had assumed.

I could see her disappointment, the frustration simmering as she looked out the window, smacking her lips, with her hands clenched in her lap. It was as if my refusal had ignited something buried in both of us. Words slipped out faster than I could rein them in, and our conversation became sharper, emotions spilling over as I tried to explain why her last-minute decision wouldn't work. I tried to keep calm and reason with her, but each word seemed to push her further away, deepening her sense of rejection. She grew increasingly upset, insisting that I should have made arrangements for her. She said I should have anticipated her needs and been ready to change everything because of who she was—my mother. But I couldn't. I had worked too hard, come too far, and built too much to upend my life without warning.

My apartment was small, my space limited, and I had to make financially sound choices that made sense for where I was in life. Having a roommate was part of my careful steps to keep myself afloat and save to buy a house soon. As much as I loved her and wanted to heal our relationship, I couldn't undo all that for a decision I hadn't even known about until that moment. Eventually, she took a long breath, eyes cast downward, and I felt the tension in the car begin to subside. She nodded slowly, quietly accepting that she would stay with my grandmother as we had originally planned. Her voice softened, and she murmured, "It's okay. I'll stay with her."

I knew it wasn't exactly okay, that it hurt her, and that it was a blow to the fragile connection we had managed to build. But in the quiet moments that followed, as we drove back to Milwaukee, I realized that maybe this was part of the journey and the process of finding common ground again. It was hard to draw a line with someone I had worked so hard to pull back into my life. But somewhere in that silence, I began to understand what Aunt Grace must have felt all those years when she had to make tough decisions to protect her peace. Boundaries weren't walls—they were bridges with limits. And sometimes, the most loving thing you can do for someone you care about is not give them everything they ask for, but what you know they truly need.

Aunt Grace loved people who hurt her, but didn't let that love destroy her. She created space for healing—even when it meant saying no. Watching her over the years, I didn't realize until now that what appeared to be toughness was actually tenderness wrapped in wisdom. That same kind of wisdom informed my decision that day. I wasn't rejecting my mother—I was preserving what we had begun to rebuild. That boundary was my way of saying: I want you here, but I also want to remain whole.

And perhaps that's what love truly is. It's not just about showing up, but also about exercising restraint when necessary. Protecting the relationship means being honest about what you can offer without losing yourself.

We weren't the same people we had been years ago, and there was still so much between us—expectations, regrets, love, and hope—all tangled together in this complex web that we were trying to unravel one strand at a time.

* * *

In the days that followed, she stayed with my grandmother as planned. She attended my graduation, and I saw the pride in her eyes—a pride that seemed to whisper, 'You did it.' It was a difficult visit in many ways, filled with old hurts and unspoken expectations. But through it all, I felt a sense of resilience, a determination to keep moving forward. We weren't a perfect family, and our relationship was far from smooth. Yet, we were trying, piece by piece, to build something meaningful, something real, even if it wasn't quite the fairytale reunion I'd once imagined.

As the days turned into weeks and the excitement of graduation faded, the rhythm of daily life resumed, but a new player entered the mix: my mother. After so many years of separation, I was trying to welcome her presence into my life in Milwaukee. It felt like a gift, a chance to finally build the bond we'd missed during my childhood. I took pride in introducing her to my friends and church community, sharing my life with her in a way I had only dreamed of doing. I saw it as an opportunity for her to meet the people who had become like family to me, for her to witness my life and perhaps, in some way, feel proud. Yet, despite the new city and fresh start, old patterns lingered like shadows, reappearing slowly, creeping in where I least expected.

At first, it was subtle. There were signs I ignored or things I brushed off, believing they would pass. However, as the weeks went by, it became clear that some habits from her life in Oakland had quietly made the journey with her, like uninvited guests slipping in. I'd fought hard to escape those very habits as a kid, building a life of stability and structure away from the chaos that addiction had brought into my early years. To see it resurface was like watching the cracks in a dam begin to form, and frustration churned inside me. I had worked too hard and sacrificed too much, and I wasn't willing to let it all be disrupted by the ghosts of the past.

* * *

After a few months in Milwaukee, my mom found her own apartment. She moved in just as the leaves turned, right before winter swept in with its icy grip. She seemed pleased with her independence and was excited about having her own space. I was glad for her, hoping that a place of her own might give her some peace, a chance to settle in, and perhaps a reason to stay away from the people who had once encouraged her worst habits. But it wasn't long before the familiar characters of her past began to circle, drawn to her new place like moths to a flame.

Whispers found their way back to me, and over time, I learned that she had reconnected with new people who enabled her addiction. The betrayal, though quiet and silent, settled in my bones. It was as if I'd invited the past back into my life, and it hurt to know she had allowed it to return, intentionally or not.

One Wednesday after church, my mom asked me for a ride home. It was something I often did. After the midweek service, the church's food pantry would open, and she, being a senior, frequently received a box of groceries to help her through the week. I happily grabbed her box and headed toward her apartment, making small talk and catching up during the ride. It was late, and the sky was black, except for the dim streetlights that cast eerie shadows on the silent sidewalks. When we reached her place, she mentioned that her stove hadn't been working since she moved in, and I offered to take a quick look, not wanting her to go without it.

We walked inside, and I placed the box of groceries on the counter before making my way to the stove. I carefully pulled it out, checked the gas line, and immediately identified the problem: the valve wasn't turned on. As I reached behind to fix it, a low, rumbling cough echoed from the back of the apartment, startling me. It was the kind of cough that belonged to a man—raspy and deep. Confused, I turned to look at my mom, who stood beside me, and at that moment, a sinking feeling gripped me.

I walked down the narrow hallway to her bedroom, following the sound of that cough, and stopped in the doorway. There, sprawled across her bed, was a man I had never seen before. He lay there, asleep, or perhaps just resting, in the space my mom had only recently made her own. My mind raced with questions—who was he, how long had he been here, and, most of all, why had my mom allowed this? A mix of anger and disappointment twisted in my stomach, a storm of emotions I could barely contain. This was supposed to be her chance for a fresh start. I had hoped that this new place in Milwaukee, this distance from her past, would give her the clean slate she desperately needed. But seeing that man lying there as if he belonged reminded me of the past I'd fought so hard to leave behind. The life I'd carved out here felt like it was slipping through my fingers, tangled up in habits and people I didn't want to be part of my world.

I looked at my mom, struggling to keep my voice steady, trying to understand how we had ended up here. I didn't want to see the old patterns resurface and didn't want to be dragged back into the pain and uncertainty I had escaped as a child. But as I stood there, my mother watching me with defiance and guilt, I realized something. She was caught, as I had once been, in a cycle that was difficult to break, a pattern that would take more than a new apartment or a new city to overcome truly.

Outrage boiled up from somewhere deep inside me, the kind that rattles every nerve and keeps the voice in your head louder than any sound in the room. The man, this stranger in my mom's bed, was staring at me, his eyes wide but empty of words, probably knowing that nothing he said would make a difference. I demanded to know who he was, why he was here, and how he thought he belonged in my mother's apartment. Before he could stammer an answer, my mom interjected, looking at me with a hardened expression, as if she were almost ready for this moment, to defend her choices. "He's my friend," she said firmly.

"Friend?" I challenged, my tone sharper than I intended. "You know him well enough to let him lie in your bed when you're not here? You barely know this man!" My words spilled out in a rush, each syllable drenched with years of frustration, anger, and, underneath it all, the worry of a son who had seen his mother entangled in darkness before. I wanted to shake her, to make her understand that she wasn't alone anymore, that she didn't have to settle for relationships or habits that only tore her down.

She glared at me, crossing her arms, then unleashed a torrent of anger and frustration. She had needs, she told me, needs I wouldn't understand. Needs she believed were her right to have, regardless of what I thought of them. There was something in her tone that cut me. It was the sound of someone who had been told for too long what they could or couldn't have, what they could or couldn't be. But that wasn't enough to excuse her behavior, not when it threatened to bring everything I'd built here crashing down. "I've worked hard to build a life here," I said, my voice tight. "You know that, and you know what I went through to get away from…from this. From these habits, these strangers in my life. Why would you bring it all back here, Mom? Why?"

The room fell silent, and for a moment, we just stared at each other, as if finally seeing one another for the first time. She didn't answer, at least not with words. The lines on her face softened, but her eyes were guarded, and I realized that she would do what she wanted, regardless of what I thought.

I knew then that this wasn't just about some man in her bed, or even the habits she had allowed to seep back into her life. It was about her painful journey, the scars she carried, and the ways she'd learned to fill those wounds, ways I couldn't always understand, even if I wanted to. And that realization left me exhausted. We were on different sides of the same chasm, and I couldn't reach her for the first time.

I walked out of her apartment that night, the slam of the door echoing like a gunshot down the quiet hallway. I left her with a few last words, blunt and unfiltered, that came from the raw ache of wanting better for her and the resignation of knowing she might not want the same for herself. It hurt to let go, to leave her there in that small apartment I had once hoped would be a sanctuary for her.

Sometimes, it's not what's said that hurts—it's the silence that follows, heavy with everything we didn't know how to say. Though spoken in anger, my words were meant to convey my love for her and my desire for her to be better than this, yet all she heard was criticism and judgment. A memory, echoing with a sound I never meant to create.

CHAPTER 17
The Voice of Silence

"There will come a time when silence is all that remains—because the truth you once rejected will stand on its own."

In the weeks that followed, we didn't talk. The silence stretched between us like a bruise that wouldn't heal. I tried to distract myself, to tell myself that it was for the best, but worry gnawed at the edges of my thoughts. I asked people at church if they'd seen her, checked in with neighbors—but no one had any news.

Only when I called my cousin's mother, who lived across the street, did I feel the first pangs of real fear. "I haven't seen her," she said, her voice soft and concerned. I knew I couldn't ignore it anymore; something wasn't right. I called my aunt in California on the phone, holding my breath while waiting for her to answer. Finally, she picked up, and the words tumbled out in a rush. "Have you heard from my mom? I haven't seen or talked to her in weeks," I said. I just wanted to know if she was safe, like any child would like for their parent. My aunt responded quickly and curtly: "I'm not getting in the middle of this, but here—I'll pass her the phone." And there it was. My mother had quietly packed up two thousand miles away, left Milwaukee without a word, and returned to California. She hadn't said goodbye, hadn't told me, and hadn't left a single sign of where she'd gone. The relief was immediate, almost dizzying. She was alive; she was safe. But beneath the relief was a hollow ache— the knowledge she had left once again, leaving nothing but silence in her place.

As I sat there, clutching the phone and listening to her breathe on the other end, I felt a strange mix of emotions—anger, sadness, but mostly disappointment—not just in her but in the life we had worked so hard to build, a life that had crumbled under the weight of our unresolved past. She had left, but maybe, in a way, we had both let go and retreated to our corners, carrying our hurt and disappointment like shields.

As we spoke, I realized that this was a crossroads. She made her choice, and though it stung, I knew I had to respect it. She needed to find her own way, no matter how winding or treacherous that path might be. In that conversation on the phone, she shared her need to get away to make a change – a long overdue change – one that would build a better future for her, but most importantly for us.

The silence between us had given her time to reflect on her choices, the distance, and the damage that had led us here. Leaving Milwaukee wasn't just an escape; it was her attempt at healing. And for the first time in our relationship, I used my voice—not to plead, but to speak a truth that had lived inside me for years: *"There will come a time when silence is all that remains— because the truth you once rejected will stand on its own."*

Addiction had been the fracture line in our lives. It was the thread behind every unstable chapter—the moves, the strange visitors, the flickering lights of disconnected power. That brokenness stole moments that should have belonged only to a mother and son. I carried the weight of abandonment, and she carried the weight of regret. Together, we lived in a reality shaped more by survival than by relationship.

In that moment, I let go of the anger and disappointment and allowed myself to love her, even in her flaws and choices, from afar. I hung up the phone, knowing that though we were miles apart, our bond was unbreakable. However complicated and painful, she was still my mom and deserved to be loved unconditionally.

THE VOICE OF SILENCE

Time flowed forward, carrying the weight of change, and my resolve to support her through her journey deepened. Whenever I could, I returned to Oakland, weaving through familiar streets to see her and witness her progress firsthand. In a moment of her liberation, I told her, 'Because of your decision, there is nothing I won't do for you now that you've turned your life around.' I truly meant those words, and I was ready to make sacrifices to ensure she was okay.

For years, her life was a constant battle—a fight she hadn't chosen but faced, nonetheless. Yet, unlike many others, her story didn't end in defeat. She made the brave decision to turn her life around, and because of that choice, I wanted her to know that she was not alone. I was determined to provide the unwavering support she needed to see her journey through, ensuring she always knew that her transformation was worth it.

Each visit became a testament to strength as the shadows of her struggles gradually lifted, revealing the woman I had always believed in—a woman of love, fierce protectiveness, unwavering faith, and boundless care. She evolved into a living example of how a life once burdened by challenges could pivot with a shift in perspective and an embrace of hope. Her strength and newfound clarity illuminated not just her path but mine, serving as a reminder that redemption and renewal are always possible.

Healing with my mother gave me something I didn't know I'd needed so deeply—a glimpse of what restoration could look like when both people were willing to try. It taught me that even the most fractured relationships could find light again. But even as that part of me was learning to trust again, another part remained quietly bruised. The boy in me—the one who used to wait by the window or listen for footsteps outside the door—was still hoping. Still believing that maybe this time, he'd show up. That a knock would come. That a smile, a hug, or even a simple "I missed you" would arrive with it. But the silence stayed. And in that silence, a different kind of ache took root.

CHAPTER 18
Waiting Patiently

"Our responsibility is to love; the only time demonstrated love ceases is in death, yet even then, our love still radiates."

The relationship between my dad and me was never straightforward. It was never a simple story of a son idolizing his father or a father being a consistent presence in his son's life. There were moments, yes, but they were scattered like fragments of a dream I could never fully piece together. Growing up, he was always there, but not always present. There's a difference between being around and truly being with someone. My dad was around, but wasn't always the dad I needed him to be.

I never grew up with the idealized version of a two-parent household. It was just me and my mom, holding down the fort and doing what needed to be done. There were other kids in the neighborhood, other families where both parents were present, and sometimes I'd find myself wondering what it must have been like to have both parents under one roof. But I didn't know any other way. We adapt. You do what you have to. My mom did her best, even with her own challenges, so it didn't seem like such a big deal then. Why was it important for me? I didn't know. As a kid, you accept your circumstances because that's what life gives you, and you learn to manage what you have.

Still, that absence was felt. I couldn't put words to it then, but there was a void—a space I wasn't sure how to fill. It lingered in the back of my mind as I navigated my days—those unspoken moments when a father's advice, guidance, or just his presence could have made all the difference.

My parents had been married once. There was an old photo album in the corner of my mind where I sometimes revisit an image of my parents' wedding day. I was barely three or four years old, but the memory is so vivid that it sometimes feels like I am still there, standing with my little, chubby hands at my sides, wearing a chocolate brown tuxedo made of polyester. I remember the ruffled cream shirt I had to wear—oh, how those shirts were everywhere in the 80s. It was the style, the trend of the time. I hated it, but it was the way of the world. I was a small, shy but outspoken boy, with my hair shaped into a little afro, looking up at the camera as if I knew what was happening but was far too young to understand.

My dad stood next to me in the same outfit, and looking at the photos, I remember thinking—I looked better. I was this adorable kid in a tuxedo. You had to love me. I admired something about that day, about the two of us standing together, and I still hold onto it. It was the last time I saw us as a family before things began to unravel. I'm told that the marriage lasted a few years, but the separation came soon after. I'm unsure what happened or if their bond was broken, but the breakup became my reality. I don't remember the specifics; it was just that one day they were together, and the next, they weren't. And that was the beginning of a new normal.

* * *

Dad worked tirelessly, dedicating his life as a sanitation worker for the City of Berkeley. Day in and day out, he cleaned the streets of the city he called home, leaving behind a legacy of hard work and pride in his community. Though it wasn't glamorous work, he did it with pride. Even after the separation, my dad remained a dedicated man, always committed to providing for me in whatever way he could. When he moved into his sister's place, I would visit him there on some weekends. His sister's apartment building was a two-story, L-shaped structure that seemed like a maze to me then. The apartment was nestled in the fold of the L, and every time I visited, I felt a strange sense of comfort and familiarity.

It was an odd little world, but it was ours. My dad's room was just off the living room, featuring a dresser and a bed that was never made—just the way I liked it. His sister, my aunt, had her space, and when I'd visit, it felt like a small village of family—my cousins' loud voices echoing through the apartment, running around as kids do, never a dull moment. I remember the little moments, like sitting at the kitchen table, eating fried bologna sandwiches with melted cheese—a simple meal that felt like a feast to my young taste buds. The bologna would sizzle in the pan until the edges were charred black, puffing up in the center. You couldn't even place it on the bread without cutting small slits so it could lay flat-topped with either Miracle Whip or mustard to suit our taste buds. I will admit, those were some of my childhood's happiest days. They were times of lightness when the weight of family struggles was a distant thought, tucked away in a corner of my mind.

We often went to San Pablo Park, just down the street. It was one of those parks with old equipment, where swings creaked as you pushed them higher and higher, feeling as if you could touch the sky. We played basketball or just ran around with no real agenda—simply enjoying the sun's warmth on our skin and the wind in our hair. It was a time of simple carefree joy when I could be a kid, and my dad—well, he was present in the way he knew how to be, even if it was just a fleeting moment of connection.

But things didn't always remain that way. Over time, the cracks in our relationship began to show. As much as my dad worked hard and provided in his own way, there were unspoken words and gaps in the space between us. I wanted something deeper than fried bologna sandwiches and park visits. I wanted to understand him better and feel he was a part of my life. However, that deeper connection was difficult to reach – until later.

As time passed, I realized that no matter how much I yearned for a more traditional father-son bond, this was something my dad could not give me, or perhaps it was something he didn't know how to provide. My relationship with him wasn't characterized by closeness or deep emotional ties. Instead, it was a series of moments—small and fleeting—some of which I held onto

WAITING PATIENTLY

while others faded into the distance. But the truth is, I did not need him to be perfect, nor did I need him to be someone he wasn't. I needed him to be there however he could, which was enough.

Alford, K. (2024) *The Little Guy* [Photograph]. Oakland, California: Keywords Unlocked, LLC

In hindsight, I realize that the love I wanted, the connection I was searching for, was always there—it just had to be understood differently. My dad may not have been around as much as I had hoped, but he did his best and cared in his own way. I recognize that sometimes, what we get from our parents isn't what we expect or want, but it's still part of the story of who we are. As I grew older, I learned to embrace those small moments, even the imperfect ones, because they shaped me into who I am today.

There came a time when the quality time that once filled the gaps of my childhood ceased to exist, and my father's promises slipped through the cracks like sand in the wind. I was too young to understand then, too naive to grasp what was happening. At that age, I believed in the magic of father-son moments—the weekends filled with laughter, trips to the park, and the feeling of safety that only a father can bring. But then came the day when everything changed, and I was left to put together pieces of a broken promise.

* * *

I remember the excitement of that Friday afternoon as if it were yesterday. I had been counting down the days all week. My dad was scheduled to pick me up after I got home from school, and I could hardly contain my anticipation. I packed my little bag the night before—an old plastic Safeway grocery bag, which was all I had. There were no duffel bags or fancy suitcases for me. I stuffed my underwear, socks, pants, and a shirt inside. Neatly folded in that thin, crinkling bag, they were ready for the weekend adventure I imagined awaited me. After school, I rushed home, my small heart thumping with excitement. I must have been in the third or fourth grade—just old enough to understand the thrill of looking forward to something, but still young enough to trust it would happen. I walked the six blocks home from school with my friends, chatting about nothing important as kids do. I remember passing the corner store where we sometimes stopped to buy garbage pail cards or chewing gum, then walking down the hill to my house. But that day, my focus was different. I had a purpose. Today, I was going to see and be with my dad.

My mom had already called him to find out if he was on the way. As she reassured me, I could hear her voice, the hope in it. "He's on his way, Key Key," she said. And so, I sat on the steps, waiting, my heart full of eager expectation. But as the minutes passed, the hours seemed to stretch, endless and heavy. The light began to fade, and the air grew cooler. The sun had set, the streetlights flickered on, and still, he was nowhere to be seen. My dad had not shown up yet.

Finally, after what felt like a lifetime, my mom came to the top of the steps; her face was a mixture of sadness and resignation. "Your dad isn't coming to get you today. Come back upstairs," she said. I sat there for a moment, frozen, as if the words were still sinking in. The excitement drained from me, replaced by a feeling I couldn't yet name—disappointment, yes, but also confusion. Why wasn't he here? Why had he promised and then broken that promise? I didn't understand, not then.

As time passed, this wasn't an isolated incident. It became the norm, and soon I realized that waiting for him was an exercise in patience that never bore fruit. The excitement I once felt in anticipation of seeing him faded into a quiet ache, a low hum in the back of my mind. The father-son moments that should have been part of my upbringing became fewer and farther between. The presence I had once craved seemed to slip away, and I learned to live without it.

* * *

As I grew older, life took me far from Oakland—over 2,000 miles away—to a new place and life where better opportunities awaited me. It wasn't just the emotional distance between us that grew; it was the physical distance. The relationship between my dad and me seemed to fade into nothingness. It felt like an absence I couldn't fill, and yet, despite it all, my love for him never wavered. It was a silent love, the kind that doesn't demand presence to exist and persists even when it feels one-sided.

But I was an adult now, and something deep inside me urged me to reach out. To find him. To rekindle what we had lost, to restore the connection that life had disrupted. I knew I had to try because it wasn't just about the relationship—it was about forgiving, understanding, and finding peace. No matter what happened, I still owed it to myself and him to give us a chance. I couldn't let the past dictate what our future might be.

Over time, our relationship improved. Slowly, like a plant growing from cracked concrete, we began to rebuild. We spent time together, sharing stories and catching up on years that had been lost. It felt good, like finally letting the sun touch a wound hidden away for so long. However, even as we began to repair the broken pieces, something inside me had changed. I was no longer the child waiting on the steps for his dad to show up. I had built walls around myself, walls that kept the hurt from cutting too deep.

I had learned to manage the pain of his absence—to survive without him in a way that allowed me to keep moving forward. When he reentered my life,

I welcomed him, but with a certain guardedness. Over time, I realized that waiting hadn't just taught me patience—it had shaped my identity. It showed me who I was without the people I longed for. Each missed visit and each unanswered promise carved something deeper in me. I stopped waiting with hope and started waiting with understanding. In that understanding, I began to become someone else. Someone stronger. Someone who knew how to stand up after being let down.

Waiting compelled me to ask: Who am I when the people I love don't show up? Who do I become when what I need never arrives? In those quiet spaces—on the porch steps, in my room, on long car rides back home—I began to shape the version of myself that would no longer be defined by what I didn't have. The boy who used to sit with a bag packed and a heart full of expectation was now a man who understood that sometimes, the waiting itself was the becoming.

But waiting didn't just shape who I was becoming—it also reshaped what I believed about people. I started to carry a quiet rule: **Don't expect too much.** Don't count on people to keep their word, because when they don't, it hurts more than not expecting anything. My dad's absence, especially when I waited and he didn't show, taught me how to lower my expectations so I wouldn't feel the sting of disappointment. It seemed safer—less painful than hoping and being let down.

But that self-protection came at a cost. I became cautious and guarded. Even when people meant well, I doubted their follow-through, not because they had failed me, but because the wound of being left waiting had trained me to expect the worst. It became a psychological weight I didn't fully understand at the time, but it followed me into friendships, relationships, and moments where trust was needed, but hesitation took the lead.

There was a new dynamic—he had returned, but I had grown into an adult who learned to navigate life on my own. I wasn't that child anymore, waiting for the promises that never came. Still, there was love between us. It wasn't the love shared between a child and his father, but love nonetheless—a bond shaped by its own meaning and depth. And in his eyes, I could see how proud he was of me. Maybe it was because I was his only son, or perhaps because he knew he hadn't been there to shape who I had become. But I could see it in how he spoke about me to others. It was a mixture of pride and lingering regret.

Looking back, I can see the complexity of it all—the absence, the disappointment, and the gradual rebuilding of our bond. I can also see how, despite everything, he shaped who I am today. His absence taught me something powerful: the value of love, unconditional and pure—the love that transcends mistakes, forgives imperfections, and moves forward without looking back.

Our relationship was never perfect, but it was mine, and it was real. I realized that love, when rooted in forgiveness and understanding, has the power to heal. The past—those broken promises and unfulfilled expectations—does not define the future. We can choose how we move forward, build relationships, and gift others the forgiveness they might not even know they need. In doing so, we free ourselves, too.

I chose to love my father unconditionally, just as I had when I was that little boy waiting on the steps. But love, I learned, isn't just a feeling we hold onto—it's a bridge we sometimes have to build with our own hands. And loving someone who let you down means showing up even when they didn't. I had carried my pain long enough. It was time to lay it down and start paving a new path—one marked not by what we lost, but by what we were still capable of building together.

CHAPTER 19
Bridging the Gaps

*"Time is one thing that you can never get back.
Take time to cherish it and the gift it gives each day."*

As an adult, I often found myself on long flights from Milwaukee to Oakland, determined to do what I could to bridge the gaps that had grown so wide between my parents and me. I did not grow up with the benefit of readily available bonds, but now, as a man, I couldn't shake the feeling that some pieces were missing, pieces only they could provide. Growing up in church, I was taught to honor my parents and uphold respect and grace so that my days might be long. It was drilled into me that it was the child's duty to enforce that reverence, even if the circumstances seemed unfair. Yet I could not always silence the voice in my mind that questioned the weight of this responsibility. Why was it on me to repair what I had not broken? Why was it my job to fix the frayed ends of a family story I had not torn?

These questions lingered, but I set them aside each year when I packed a bag, booked the flight, and rented a car to make my pilgrimage back to Oakland. No matter what, I didn't want my life to end with regrets. I wanted to say that I had done my part to "make it work." Even though I had fled Oakland years ago to escape hardship, those streets held a mirror to my life, reflecting both who I was and who I was striving to become.

Each visit was bittersweet, pulling me back into my past with a mix of pride and trepidation. I drove through old neighborhoods, tracing the paths I had once taken as a child on my bike, now with the confidence of a grown man. The buildings were the same, stoic as ever, with stories etched in their peeling paint and cracked sidewalks. Each corner held some stark and painful memories, while others were joyful. I allowed these memories to flood back, reminding me of what I had overcome. They played like scenes in a movie only I could see, each one underscoring the odds I had beaten, the statistics I had refused to become.

Finding my mom had always been easier than reconnecting with my dad. She stayed in touch with family, and we began to rebuild as our conversations grew over the years. There was something deeply healing in those heart-to-heart conversations, even if they were difficult. We did not always see eye-to-eye on who was responsible for what happened in the past, but we reached an understanding that allowed us to move forward. I rented a car each time I visited, and sometimes I stayed with her in her modest one-bedroom apartment in West Oakland. She lived in a senior citizen complex, where her cozy space became our meeting ground. She maintained a small balcony, where she would feed the birds every morning—a quiet routine that gave her peace.

Though small, her apartment had the comfort of a well-lived home. The TV flickered with her favorite shows, especially her beloved "Young & the Restless." She had followed those soap operas religiously for as long as I could remember; the faces on the screen were like family to her, as familiar as her own. When I stayed, she worried about me constantly, reminding me to be careful in the streets, just as she had when I was a child. It didn't matter that I was a grown man; she was still the mother, as protective as ever.

Our visits weren't always easy. As much as we loved each other, there were still old habits and patterns that sometimes pulled us apart. I encouraged her to make better decisions and let go of some things that had hurt her in the past, but she was stubborn. When she didn't agree with my advice, she would put her foot down in the way only she could, saying, "I'm the momma. I had you; you didn't have me." The phrase always made me smile, her way of reminding me who was in charge. I respected her, even if we disagreed. And she usually came around over time, realizing I was only trying to do what was best for her.

Each trip to Oakland left me with mixed emotions. I wanted to savor our time together, but could not ignore the struggles that sometimes resurfaced. Still, we were working on it, finding new ways to connect and bridge that gap between the past and the present. In these visits, I did not just rediscover my mom; I rediscovered parts of myself, finding the strength to forgive and love despite the years of distance and hurt.

* * *

Whenever I visited Oakland, I was determined to find my dad. However, searching for him in those early trips felt like chasing shadows. I would receive vague reports from family and friends: "We just saw him by San Pablo Park," or "He was on Market Street the other day." They all led to dead ends. My dad, now retired, did not have a routine that anyone could pinpoint, and there was no permanent place where I could be certain of finding him. Each time I returned to Oakland, I took my chances, hoping this would be the trip when fate would finally bring us together. And at last, one day, it did.

Before this visit, I learned he had remarried and lived in East Oakland with Karen, his new wife. The news shocked me, but it also sparked a quiet happiness within me, a hope that this new chapter had brought him stability and perhaps even someone who could positively influence us both. I entered that visit with optimism, imagining what it would be like to finally have the face-to-face connection I had been waiting for.

When I arrived, the sun hung high in a clear California sky. I parked my car at the base of a small hill, looking up at a four-unit apartment complex nestled behind a flowerbed dotted with succulents and a few tall, scraggly trees. The slight incline of the street added a certain character, reminiscent of a scene from an old movie set in Oakland's East Side. His unit was on the left, behind a black, slightly worn screen door that rattled in the blowing wind. With the bay only a few miles away, the air was warm yet carried that familiar Bay Area freshness.

I knocked on the screen door, the sound echoing loudly through the stillness of the house as if the door hadn't been used often or was about to fall off its hinges. The noise carried through the apartment, and soon, someone came to answer. It was Karen. She looked at me with a warm, open expression, and I noticed right away that she wasn't Black; she was Hispanic, with a friendly yet guarded look in her eyes. Her gaze softened when I introduced myself, and with a smile, she invited me in, saying, "Come on in; he's been waiting for you."

Inside, the apartment was dimly lit yet cozy in its own way, with the faint smell of fresh coffee and aging paper. There he was, sitting on a modest couch that had experienced its fair share of life, just as he had. When he saw me, he stood up with a hint of surprise and pride in his eyes. It had been years since we last saw each other, but he looked just as I remembered—aged, yes, but still unmistakably my dad. He was tall, around 6'4", with broad shoulders that suggested a lifetime of hard work, no doubt from his years as a sanitation worker. His skin was a rich, mocha brown, marked with subtle signs of age, yet his face still conveyed the familiar strength I remembered from childhood.

He reached out to shake my hand, and as he pulled me in for a hug, I noticed the neat buzz of his gray beard, meticulously trimmed, framing his face with a quiet dignity. He wore a plaid button-up shirt, fastened neatly at the top, and a pair of navy blue khakis. At that moment, I was hit by a wave of nostalgia; he looked strong and steady, as if he had been chiseled by life's demands but hadn't let them break him.

I sat in a well-worn armchair, its fabric stretched and faded from years of use. Around me, the living room was cluttered with papers, bags, and boxes stacked haphazardly yet carefully—evidence of lives lived with little room to let go of things, but not quite at the level of hoarding. It was disordered, yet purposeful, as though everything had meaning or a story. A narrow path wound between the stacks, just enough room to move around, and it was clear that this space held a lifetime of collected memories, items too sentimental to throw away.

As we began to talk, I felt a mix of emotions swirling inside me—relief, curiosity, and a lingering hesitation about what he would say or how he would react to my questions. I shared updates about my life in Milwaukee—about work and school—and he listened thoughtfully, nodding occasionally as he absorbed it all. He shared a bit about his current days and how he spent most of his time staying busy, still managing to fit in some exercise when he could.

The rhythm of our conversation was gentle, filled with pauses as we both found our footing in this new territory of father and son trying to reconnect. I studied his face as he spoke, noticing the small creases at the corners of his eyes and the way his gaze drifted now and then, as though lost in his thoughts. For a moment, he was just my dad, no longer the elusive figure I had spent years trying to find, but a man with his own story, his own struggles, and the faint hope that maybe we could carve out something meaningful from the time we had.

Alford, K. (2018) *Dad* [Photograph]. Oakland, California: Keywords Unlocked, LLC

BRIDGING THE GAPS

The visit was brief, but it felt significant. Sitting there, surrounded by his apartment's cluttered yet comforting chaos, I realized that this was a piece of him—a piece I had missed. Yet here it was, waiting for me to find it. As I left, I carried a sense of peace with me, knowing that no matter how far apart we had drifted, I had finally found my dad.

For years, my trips to California followed a steady routine. I'd fly into town, see my dad, and sit down to discuss life—the usual updates, sprinkled with the familiar gaps in our relationship. Our phone calls between these visits were sparse on both ends. Life kept me busy with work and travel in Milwaukee, while he was content in his retired routine. Often, it wasn't even him calling directly; Karen would be on the line, saying, "Hey, Keyimani, your dad wants to talk to you." She'd ask me how I was doing, but it was always brief and felt like small talk. There was an undercurrent of tension between us, unspoken but palpable, and as the years went on, it began to surface more directly.

In time, our conversations began to involve frequent disagreements. She felt strongly that I should make more of an effort to reach out and check on him. I understood her perspective, but her approach stung, especially given how little she knew about the complicated history between my dad and me. Here I was, putting in the effort I could—making trips from Milwaukee and always being the one to initiate contact. Despite living just a plane ride away, my dad had never come to visit me, even after all these years. But I accepted it; I wanted to build a connection with him as an adult, and if that meant shouldering most of the responsibility, I did so, even if it didn't feel entirely fair.

One trip stood out: a visit when we discussed him finally coming to see me in Milwaukee. He seemed genuinely interested, and I could feel the excitement. I wanted to share my life with him, show him what I had built for myself—the house I had bought, my car, and the city that had shaped me. We planned it around his birthday, and I was thrilled. It would be his first time in Milwaukee to see another part of the world outside California and Louisiana. But when the time came, everything fell apart. His trip was suddenly off the table, replaced by a new plan. Karen and my dad decided to go to Disneyland instead. My heart sank.

As he explained, my mind drifted back to childhood, to the days I'd waited for him, promises left unfulfilled while waiting alone on the steps. This time, though, I placed the blame squarely on her. She had convinced him to abandon our plans, trading what could have been a moment of father-son bonding for a trip to Disneyland. That disappointment weighed on me, deepening our already strained relationship.

From that moment on, our interactions became more strained. Whenever I called, I braced myself, hoping she wouldn't answer. When she did, there was little I wanted to discuss with her. I felt she didn't like me; truthfully, the feeling was mutual. I didn't like this animosity, but it was clear that she wasn't invested in building anything meaningful with me. When Christmas and birthdays came around, I'd send my dad gifts as a small gesture, reminding him I was still thinking of him. I wanted a positive relationship with my father, but she was the wall keeping us apart.

Things escalated one day when she crossed a line and made some disparaging comments about my mom. I could feel the anger rising within me, and I firmly put her in her place. My mom was off-limits. From then on, we barely acknowledged each other's existence, and honestly, it was a relief.

* * *

As the years slipped by, my dad's health began to decline. Whenever I received a call about his health, I dropped everything and booked the first flight to California to be by his side. One year, I got a call telling me he'd had a stroke. A wave of dread washed over me, and without a second thought, I made my way to Oakland. I arrived at Kaiser Permanente in West Oakland, a hospital close to where my family had once lived. Upon walking in, I went to the registration desk and asked for his room number, my pulse quickening with worry. When I entered the room, he was alone. The sight of him lying there, his body curled slightly to one side, hit me hard. His face bore the visible effects of the stroke—the left side sagged somewhat, his mouth partially open, and his speech was slurred, each word coming with effort. Despite the sadness, I felt relieved that he was still here. I could still talk to him and be there for him, which was what mattered most at that moment. But a question lingered in the back of my mind, gnawing at me. Why was he alone? Where was his wife? I finally asked him, "Where is Karen?" He told me she had gone to Sacramento to visit her family. My heart sank. How could she leave him now, in his time of need? It was a betrayal of the commitment they had made to each other. Weren't the vows meant to carry them through moments like this? I couldn't believe she would abandon him after a stroke, a life-altering event. But I swallowed my anger and put it aside, reminding myself he needed my strength now more than ever.

I stayed for a week, adjusting my work schedule and putting everything else on hold. I did what I could to lift his spirits by sitting by his bedside and helping him through the little daily hurdles that had become enormous challenges due to his condition. When I finally had to leave, he was discharged the following day, but I knew that his recovery would be a long and difficult road.

* * *

After that, I regularly checked on him, calling often and doing whatever I could to ensure he knew I was there. It wasn't easy to navigate a relationship that had been so fractured for so long. But even though the miles separated us, and despite the many things that had tried to drive a wedge between us, I still wanted to be there to give him the love that only a son could provide.

Through all the hurt, distance, quiet moments, and awkward conversations, I learned most from those visits that family doesn't have to be perfect to matter. We can't change the past, but we can choose how we carry it. Forgiveness wasn't just about letting him off the hook; it was about letting go of the heavy expectations I had been holding onto. Giving grace didn't erase the pain, but it made room for something better to grow.

For a long time, I believed love had to be perfect, close, consistent, and always present. However, I started to realize that love can thrive in broken places. It can manifest in the effort, the return, and the sincere attempts to make things right. That type of love doesn't remove the hurt, but it aids in healing it. It reminded me that someone's worth isn't defined by their perfection but by their place in your heart—even with their flaws.

OAKLAND HILLS, MILWAUKEE RIVERS

But even as we slowly rebuilt something worth holding onto, life—unpredictable and unrelenting—had its own timeline. Just as we were learning to navigate each other with more grace than resentment, a new reality confronted us—one that would demand presence over promises, forgiveness over frustration, and love not as an idea but as an act of goodbye.

CHAPTER 20
The Final Goodbye

"Chapters close, and life often finds ways to remind us of its contents. Remember them and ensure that each word amplifies its purpose."

Over the years, my dad's health slowly slipped. Diabetes clung to him, a quiet but relentless thief, eroding his strength and endurance. It was a slow war with his own body, and it was one that he was losing. Every visit to California reminded me of how much frailer he had become. I could see it in his legs, where poor circulation had begun to take its toll. There came a day on one of those trips when he had to make a choice that I knew cut to his core—whether or not to undergo surgery on his foot. The tissue was dying, blackening with gangrene that spread in dark strokes across his skin. If he left it, his body would slowly poison itself. Surgery was the only way. But to him, this wasn't a mere procedure. It was the forced surrender of something he had long held sacred: his ability to walk normally.

Walking had been his strength, his sense of freedom, as deeply a part of him as anything else. It was his therapy, exercise, independence, and way of conquering the world around him. Walking made him feel powerful—like Samson with his hair, strength rooted in something sacred. The thought of losing it struck at something fundamental within him, as if he were being asked to give up part of his own identity. After hours of conversation and reflection, he agreed to surgery. He made the sacrifice for his health—but the cost weighed on both of us in ways that neither of us could fully express.

* * *

In December 2017, the call came again. This time, though, it was different—his voice wasn't on the other end. Someone else shared the news: he wasn't doing well. He was in hospice. I barely grasped what hospice meant then. I assumed it was just another round of treatment, some help for his recovery, not the final stage it so often signals. I'd learn soon enough.

It was nearly time for winter break, ten days of the year when the campus closed and work paused. But none of that mattered now. Within hours, I booked a flight, packed hastily, and was on a plane to California early the next morning. Upon arrival, I went straight to the facility, near the one he had been in after the amputation. The place was just down the street from where I had visited him last. Everything about it felt all too familiar. I walked through those hallways that reeked of antiseptic and time, and a nurse escorted me to his room.

* * *

When I walked in, I saw him lying there, half-asleep, a shell of the man he had once been. The father I'd looked up to, the one I'd seen as a hero, seemed small, as though his strength had leaked out of him and left only shadows. There he was, in bed, lying on his side, slightly resembling himself. He was alone in the room; Karen had left to return to the house for a while. I sat in the chair beside his bed and waited, hardly breathing myself, afraid that even a whisper might break something precious.

Eventually, he stirred, and I saw the flicker of recognition in his eyes as he looked at me. His face softened, and a smile bloomed, faint but warm, as he held out his hand. "I knew you'd be here," he said, his voice like gravel underfoot—worn and shaky but sure. "I knew my son would come to see me." I took his hand, pressing it in mine, feeling its familiar weight and the loss of strength I hadn't noticed before. I smiled back, trying hard not to let the tears well up. My dad, my hero, was lying in a bed, slipping away a little more with each passing day.

THE FINAL GOODBYE

The days that followed were measured in small breaths, gentle conversations, and silences that felt as heavy as conversations once had, all part of a rhythm that would stay with me forever. Each word he spoke seemed to cost him something—his breath would hitch, and his body would tremble with the effort of each sound. Every sentence felt like a slow climb, but he kept going. When he rested, I'd sit beside him, watching him drift between sleep and wakefulness, trying to memorize every feature and every expression.

I fed him when he had the strength to eat, watched him rest as his strength waned, and every so often, he'd talk. Some of our conversations took me back—he spoke of regrets, of the mistakes he'd made, and then he'd turn to me, with eyes filled with a love I knew but rarely heard spoken aloud, "I'm proud of you, son," he'd tell me, his voice thick with emotion, "proud to see the man you've become." And when the nurses came by, he'd look to them and tell them, too, his voice brightening a little. "This is my son," he'd say, "he's a doctor."

As the days progressed towards me needing to leave, he found ways to tell me how much I meant to him, and I could feel the weight of those words fill the space between us. I stayed there for ten days, each moment feeling like a precious gift, yet I knew the time would come when I'd have to go back home. By my tenth day there, the nurses told me he would go home soon. I took that as a sign he was getting better. It was hope, naïve but sincere, and I clung to it as I said goodbye, promising to call and check in. When I left, I still believed that we had more time.

*　*　*

It was the early hours of a quiet Monday morning, around 4:00 a.m. The sky outside my window was still dark, thick with the silence that only comes before dawn. Tomorrow would be the first day of the spring semester at work, and I had planned to rest, to gather my strength for the busy week ahead. But the shrill ring of my cell phone shattered the stillness, cutting through my sleep like a sharp breath of cold air. My phone lay on the nightstand, its screen illuminating the darkness as it buzzed insistently, jolting me awake. I rarely woke up for phone calls, but something about this one felt different. I reached out to answer it, but the ringing stopped before my hand could reach the phone. A voicemail alert popped up, and I saw it was from California. My heart clenched.

The message was short but heavy with foreboding: "Hi, Keyimani, it's Karen. Call me, it's about your dad." Those few words struck me like a wave crashing against a rock. I fumbled to dial her back, my mind racing with possibilities, each worse than the last. When she picked up, her voice was low and weighted with sorrow. "Your dad stopped breathing in his sleep," she said softly, words falling like stones into the hollow silence. "He passed away. I'm so sorry." I sat there, motionless, my world shrinking to the narrow space between me and that phone. The words barely registered, as if they were foreign or spoken in a language I didn't understand. My mind struggled to grasp them, to believe them. The man I had just seen, the man who, despite his illness, still felt larger than life, was gone.

It felt like a cruel joke—one I desperately wanted to wake up from. I tried to respond, but no words came. She continued to explain her plans, detailing how she was arranging for his cremation and intended to hold a service in a few months. My mind cleared, sharpened by a surge of desperation. "Please," I said, voice hoarse, "don't do anything with his body until I get there. I need to see him. I need to say goodbye."

When I hung up, time seemed to stretch out, its usual flow suspended in the haze of shock and disbelief. I sat on the edge of my bed, numb, my heart heavy and swollen. Tears streamed down my face, unbidden, as I grappled with the reality of his absence. How could he be gone? How could the man I'd just held, just spoken with, now be... gone? But through the numbness, I felt the urgency rising. I needed to get to California to see him one last time. The thought of my dad reduced to ashes, his presence slipping away before I could say goodbye, filled me with fierce resolve. I couldn't let that happen. I wouldn't.

As the morning broke, I moved through the motions of calling family members, sharing the news with the hollow voice of someone barely able to comprehend it himself. The hours trickled by until I finally found a flight out of Chicago O'Hare for Tuesday morning. Without hesitation, I packed, threw on a jacket, and set out on the dark, winding drive from Madison to

THE FINAL GOODBYE

Chicago. With each mile, my mind drifted to my father—memories of his laughter, his strength, and the way he'd look at me with pride in his eyes. I was still processing it all, my thoughts spinning through grief, anger, and helplessness. I called Karen on the road to let her know I was coming, asking her again to ensure the funeral home held off on cremation. She seemed determined to rush the process, and I couldn't understand why. My frustration simmered with the thought of losing this last chance, this final moment, gnawing at me. If I couldn't see him one last time, if I couldn't look upon his face, it would be as though a part of him, a part of our story, would be forever lost. It wasn't just closure I needed—it was the chance to honor him, to hold his memory close before letting him go.

* * *

The miles passed beneath me in a blur, the road stretching endlessly before me and carrying me toward a goodbye I was still trying to find the courage to face. The moment I stepped off the plane in Oakland, the weight of why I was there pressed down on me—unshakable, heavy, and all-consuming. I barely registered the airport around me as I rushed to get my rental car, desperate yet dreading the final drive to San Leandro. The road stretched out in front of me, each passing mile feeling longer than the last. Every thought running through my mind was a question I didn't know how to answer. How would I feel when I saw him? Would I fall apart, or could I hold myself together?

On the way, I called my Aunt Cheryl. She had been a steady presence in my life, a source of comfort through many storms. When she offered to meet me at the funeral home, I hesitated. I'd always prided myself on being strong, someone who could handle life's harshest moments. But before I could politely refuse, she insisted. "You don't have to do this alone," she said firmly. I was grateful. We arrived at almost the same time, parking on the curb outside the unfamiliar building. The California sky was overcast, thick gray clouds looming as if the world understood the moment's gravity. It mirrored the heaviness in my heart.

* * *

OAKLAND HILLS, MILWAUKEE RIVERS

We walked together into the funeral home. The atmosphere was thick and quiet, filled with the muted sounds of people whispering and shuffling behind closed doors. I approached the desk and introduced myself, my voice sounding foreign and distant in my ears. After a nod of acknowledgment, the receptionist asked me to wait while they prepared my dad's body.

Standing there, I reflected on another time I'd waited like this, to see my grandmother after she'd passed. But this was different. This was my dad—the man who, despite the twists and turns in our relationship, was still my father, my first hero. The man who, even with our complications, loved me and showed it in the ways he knew best. The realization that this was the last time I'd see him in the flesh settled like a heavy stone in my stomach. I couldn't shake the fear of how I'd react, but I knew this was a moment I had to face.

The staff eventually led us to a pair of old, creaking wooden doors at the back. My Aunt Cheryl placed her arm around my shoulders, grounding me, and whispered that it was okay to cry and feel everything. "You're human," she reminded me, and I held onto her words as the doors opened.

And there he was. My dad lay on a cold table in the middle of the room. He was wrapped in clear plastic, his pale skin dotted with beads of moisture, adjusting to the room's warmth. He looked at peace, just like he had when I'd visited him in the hospital. But this time, his chest wasn't rising and falling. It was unnaturally still, a stillness that drove the truth home. My dad was gone.

A rush of grief hit me, fierce and unyielding, and before I knew it, tears poured down my face. I tried to wipe them, but they kept coming, flowing freely as I stood there, watching him. I reached out, my hand trembling as I touched his face, feeling the cold of his skin beneath my fingers. I had to see him. I had to touch him. My heart needed to understand what my mind still refused to accept fully.

I ran my hand over his head, remembering the last time I'd shaved it for him in the hospital—when he could still speak, when we could still laugh, when goodbye didn't feel so final. That moment in hospice had been sacred, but this... this was something different. This was goodbye in its truest form. He couldn't respond, but I felt something settle in touching him. It was as if my soul needed to feel his presence one last time—to say, *I was here. You were seen. You were loved.*

In that quiet moment, I became the last person to witness him—to stand beside him before he was cremated, before the rituals and ceremonies began. A funeral couldn't give me this. A memorial couldn't give me this. Only his presence could. And as the room's stillness enveloped me, I realized that even in silence, the body remembers. Touch became the language when words no longer worked. And in that touch, I found the closure I didn't know I needed.

Still, the realization gripped me—this was a goodbye I could never undo. My dad was truly gone, and this chapter of my life, our life together, was now sealed. As I stood there, my heart broken and my eyes filled with tears, I knew that I would carry this moment with me always. This was my final memory of him, a memory filled with love, pain, and the understanding that some goodbyes are final.

I walked out of that room carrying the weight of that moment. Losing him forced me to confront the fragility of time and how quickly everything can change. What I didn't know was that life wasn't done teaching me about that kind of fragility—because soon, it wouldn't be his life on the line. It would be mine.

CHAPTER 21
A Wake-Up Call

"Life or death lies in your decision; you'll either decide to choose yourself or choose others. Whatever the choice, the outcome is on you."

At fourteen, I entered the working world—driven by a relentless determination to overcome the many obstacles that had colored my upbringing in California. I had witnessed hardships that most kids my age couldn't fathom, but my Aunt Grace stepped in like a beacon of hope, ensuring that I had the essentials—food, clothes, shelter, and a semblance of stability. To me, this was a luxury. I appreciated everything she provided, not fully grasping the complexities of life at that age. After all, at fourteen, how much could I know? I was just a young Black kid, deeply involved in church activities, blissfully ignorant of the weighty matters that often plagued the minds of adults. What I wanted more than anything was the freedom of having my own money—a few dollars in my pocket to spend on whatever caught my fancy. Thus began my foray into the world of work, a venture that would extend into a career spanning nearly three decades.

Over the years, I cultivated a robust work ethic and a commitment to my responsibilities that became the hallmark of my character. I consistently showed up, poured my heart into my tasks, and often took on more than my fair share. I thrived on being busy, relishing the rush that came from balancing work, school, and church commitments. This was my routine, a frenetic cycle that filled my days with purpose, albeit at the cost of my well-being. My aunt would frequently caution me, "Keyimani, you're doing too much! One day, you're going to have a breakdown!" I would laugh it off, brushing aside her concerns with youthful bravado, assuring her that I was perfectly fine. Yet, the truth was that I wasn't okay. I often found myself teetering on the edge of exhaustion, trapped by the weight of my commitments. I had yet to grasp the concept of limits, of knowing when to say no. I was still in the process of discovering who I was, often living to fulfill the dreams and expectations of others. At the same time, my own identity lay buried beneath layers of obligation.

My first job lasted six years; my second job was an impressive fourteen. After that, I spent nearly four years at another company, and now I find myself in my current position, entering the eighth year. Throughout this journey, I juggled odd jobs like cleaning an office building during second shift while attending college full-time and working a part-time job. Perhaps I was a bit too ambitious, striving to prove myself in every capacity. I even took a telemarketing job, attempting to sell alarm systems to uninterested customers. That experience taught me a harsh lesson about human nature—how cruel people can be when they are not interested in what you're selling. Yet, despite the challenges, I maintained my employment through nearly thirty years of hard work and sacrifice, a choice I made willingly.

* * *

Years later, during a routine doctor's visit, I was met with a familiar refrain echoing my aunt's warnings: "You need to slow down and take care of yourself." This time, however, his words carried an urgency. "You have high cholesterol," he informed me. "You should consider taking medication," I remember rolling my eyes at the suggestion. I was in my late twenties, bursting with life. The idea of taking medication for the rest of my life felt absurd. I thought, "Can't I just pray about this? God can heal me!" My faith ran deep, and I believed fervently that my devotion would shield me from such mundane concerns. Yet, in my naiveté, I failed to realize that our healing often requires action. I rejected his advice and chose to ignore the warning, believing I was fine, even as the whispers of his concerns lingered in the back of my mind.

* * *

At thirty-seven, the reality of aging began to seep into my bones like a quiet, unwelcome guest. I had always been the kind of guy who moved through life with a youthful energy, a certain ease from being in my prime. But now, with each passing year, that vitality seemed to slip away just a little more. My body, once a seamless instrument of movement and strength, was starting to protest in ways I hadn't expected. Yet, time—relentless and unforgiving—waited for no one. So, I pressed on, determined to embrace life, and experience the world in new ways.

This particular chapter of my life unfolded during an event I had eagerly anticipated for months. One of my closest friends was about to get married, and as the best man, I had a role to play in the celebration of his union. A group of us—old friends who had seen each other through thick and thin and some new ones —gathered in Miami, a city of sun-soaked streets and endless possibilities. I had been to Miami before, and I knew it was the perfect spot for us to unwind before our cruise to the Bahamas.

* * *

The day was flawless. The sun beat down from a cloudless sky, and the sticky warmth of the Florida air wrapped around us like a thick, humid blanket. It was one of those days when everything seemed right. Laughter echoed through the air as we shared stories, caught up on life, and reveled in the comfort of friendship—the kind of friendship that felt timeless. One of my friends had secured a beautiful hotel room overlooking the beach, and stepping onto that balcony was like stepping into another world. The view—stretching from the golden sands of the beach to the endless horizon—felt surreal, almost dreamlike. It was paradise, and for a moment, I felt as though I could stay there forever.

As we basked in the scenery, we decided to take a stroll down Collins Avenue. The street was lined with sleek high-rise hotels and luxury apartments, the kind that promised an existence of effortless wealth. Yachts docked by the canal, their polished surfaces gleaming in the sun, stood as a silent testament to the affluent lifestyle of those who called Miami home. As we walked, the energy was infectious—laughter and stories filled the air, and for a moment, we felt invincible.

Then, suddenly, something shifted. The heat that had seemed so inviting moments ago became suffocating. I began to feel a strange warmth, an overwhelming heat that seemed to rise from within, not from the sun. I tried to brush it off, blaming the 90-degree weather for the discomfort. But as we continued walking, it only grew worse, and I found myself struggling to breathe. Something wasn't right. It felt as though the air itself had turned against me, pressing in on my chest.

I couldn't take it anymore. I needed to find shelter, to escape the unbearable heat. The nearest building was a hotel, and I practically stumbled through the doors, desperate for the cool embrace of air conditioning. To my right, near the check-in desk, I spotted some chairs—just the right place to catch my breath. The battle inside my mind began as I sank into one of the seats. This was supposed to be a celebration, the start of a memorable trip, but here I was, struggling with a foreign and all-consuming heat.

My friends, ever watchful, gathered around me, their faces etched with concern. "Are you okay?" they asked, their voices laced with worry. I forced a smile, trying to downplay it. "Yeah, I just need a cold towel," I said, though inside, I wasn't sure what was happening. Maybe it was the "special candy" we'd eaten earlier, or perhaps it was just the toll of the trip catching up with me. Whatever it was, I just wanted to feel normal again.

One of the hotel staff members quickly returned with a cold towel, which I pressed to my bald head. The chill from the towel provided a small relief, a flicker of comfort amid the heat that had overtaken my body. I sat there for what felt like an eternity, though it was probably only ten minutes. My friends hovered nearby, checking in on me, their faces filled with concern. Gradually, the heat began to subside, and the sweat that had clung to my skin evaporated. The world around me seemed to regain its usual clarity, and the heavy weight of discomfort lifted. I was okay now, but I decided to head back to the room. The air conditioner was a siren call, and I needed to rest. Perhaps planning this trip, as the best man, had drained me more than I realized. I decided it was better to take a step back and recover, to rest and regroup.

That day, I spent the afternoon under the cool hum of the air conditioner, my mind spinning with thoughts of the night ahead and the adventures yet to come. The remainder of our trip was blissful—no more unexpected bouts of heat, just good friends, good times, and memories that would last a lifetime. But for some reason, that moment in the hotel, when the heat overtook me and I thought briefly that I might ruin the trip, stayed with me. It lingered in the back of my mind, like a warning I couldn't quite shake, a reminder that things weren't always as simple as they seemed. But for now, I pushed it away and chose to enjoy the present while not knowing what would happen shortly.

* * *

One sweltering Saturday morning, I awoke feeling uncharacteristically hot, again. The summer air outside was pleasant, but something felt off within the confines of my apartment. As I sat on the edge of my bed, sweat streamed down my face as if I had just finished a jog. "What is happening to me?" I wondered, puzzled and alarmed, as this seemed familiar. With the air conditioning off and the fan idle, I decided I needed to cool down, so I went to the thermostat.

The layout of my apartment was a bit peculiar—a closet connected the bedroom to the bathroom, and after passing through, I would find the front door and the laundry space. I trudged toward the thermostat, feeling increasingly weak with each step. The switch felt heavy beneath my finger, as if unseen forces held it down. Summoning every ounce of strength, I finally managed to click it on, letting out a sigh of relief. "I'm going to be okay," I thought. But as I turned to return to my bedroom, fatigue washed over me like a wave, and I knew I needed to sit down. I slumped against the wall in my closet, my energy fading rapidly. In that dim space, surrounded by the muted colors of my clothes, anxiety began to bubble within me. "Calm down, Keyimani. Just breathe," I whispered to myself, attempting to regain control. I sat there for what felt like an eternity—10 to 15 minutes—before the echo of my doctor's warning resurfaced: "Not taking this medicine is not a matter of if; it's a matter of when." At that moment, clarity struck like lightning. Shit! I think I might be having a heart attack.

Fear gripped me, but I knew I had to act. Alone in my apartment, panic threatened to consume me. After a few moments of contemplation, I pushed myself off the floor and decided to seek help. I recalled a nearby clinic that accepted my insurance and resolved to get there. I turned on the shower, letting cold water wash over me as I sat on the built-in stool, breathing deeply to collect my thoughts. I told myself I had to be strong enough to get dressed and drive to the doctor.

Once I emerged from the shower, I felt a renewed sense of purpose. Ignoring the "what ifs," I dressed quickly, grabbed my keys, and headed out the door. The clinic was about three miles away but felt like a monumental journey. As I drove, I kept telling myself, "You need to get there." After six or seven minutes, I arrived, parking hastily and rushing inside. I explained my situation to the receptionist, and within moments, a nurse ushered me back for treatment. The words that followed confirmed my worst fears: "Keyimani, you are having a heart attack. We are calling an ambulance!"

Stunned, I stood there in disbelief. "How could this be happening?" I thought. My mind raced with questions—What does this mean for my life? My work? My church? My commitments? I felt as if the ground beneath me were crumbling. I couldn't slow down, not now, not when there was so much to do.

In that moment of crisis, I realized that life has a peculiar way of forcing us to slow down. We often face a choice: we can either pause and reflect, or life will do it for us, often in dramatic and painful ways.

That day forced me to make a decision I had spent years avoiding. I had to choose myself—not just in theory, but in practice. Choosing myself meant recognizing that I couldn't keep living to meet everyone else's needs while ignoring my own. It meant understanding that survival wasn't the same as healing. I had spent so long proving I was dependable, capable, and strong that I forgot to make space for peace. This wake-up call wasn't just about my health; it was about my worth. Moving forward, I knew I had to start protecting my future like I had always protected others.

The decision to care for ourselves rests in our hands, but the consequences of living or dying are inescapable. I understand that contributing to the things that matter is important, but it should never overshadow our ability to live fully and joyfully. I'm still learning that lesson—how to shift my perspective, even when the choices are hard. Life is a precious gift, and every moment should be cherished, lived intentionally, and embraced with a heart open to the possibilities that lie ahead.

Surviving that moment didn't just change how I saw myself—it reshaped how I saw everyone around me. Life had stripped away my excuses and forced me to pay attention to what truly mattered: the people, the memories, the lessons I had carried but hadn't yet understood. Healing wasn't just about moving forward; it was about looking back, with honesty and grace, at the ones who shaped, scarred, and saved me. Before stepping into what was next, I had to reflect on where I came from—and the ones who loved me through it all.

CHAPTER 22
Reflections

"Scars, once symbols of pain, can, with the right perspective, become signs of survival and proof of endurance, healing, and growth."

Over the years, relationships that were once fragile and strained have transformed into profound connections, forged by understanding and love. Childhood often shields us from the unseen battles our parents fight—the sleepless nights spent worrying about rent, and the sacrifices made to put food on the table. My mother's journey was no exception. Through her struggles, she became a living testament to the consequences of our choices and the possibility of redemption. She taught me that even when life feels like a labyrinth of missteps, it can still lead to a better path.

Once riddled with conflict and pain, our relationship has grown into something extraordinary—a bond so strong that the hard days feel like faded memories, serving only as a backdrop to the beauty we've built together. The love we now share is not just a gift but a choice, one we reaffirm daily. It's a reminder that parents are not perfect but precious, deserving of our gratitude and love in a way that mirrors the efforts they've made for us.

Together, we've transformed ordinary moments into extraordinary adventures—road trips that took us across landscapes and into a deeper understanding of each other. Every memory feels like a stroke on a shared canvas, where we are both artists crafting the masterpiece of our relationship. Each choice and gesture added texture, creating a more vibrant and meaningful picture over time.

The obstacles that once seemed insurmountable now lie far behind us. They have been replaced by a profound sense of peace and fulfillment. What we've created together is more than just a relationship; it's an enduring testament to resilience and love. With God's guidance, the chaos of the past has transformed into clarity and the pain into purpose.

Being a strong father requires a kind of resilience that often goes unrecognized, especially in a world where numerous forces challenge the very essence of fatherhood. The father-son bond is sacred yet fraught with complexities, shaped by unspoken expectations and deep-rooted hopes. To claim any father-son relationship is flawless would be far from the truth. True strength lies in embracing those imperfections, viewing them as opportunities to draw closer rather than as wedges to drive us apart. Reconciliation, I've learned, is a choice—a personal decision to say, 'I want this to work.' It's a step taken not out of duty, but out of a profound desire to strengthen the bond, allowing it to flourish beyond the weight of expectations or past mistakes.

My father and I walked that path, carving out time to build our relationship one moment at a time. Each memory was an investment—a conscious decision to put love at the center. As he grew older and his presence faded, our commitment to each other never waned. We built a world within those moments—a place where we could laugh until we cried, share our fears and dreams, and swap stories we kept only for each other. Most importantly, we said "I love you" often and without hesitation, letting the simplicity of those words carry the weight of everything we felt.

In a way, those memories feel like a precious inheritance. They serve as proof of a journey marked by resilience and love—a journey where we both learned that true strength lies not in appearing unbreakable but in embracing the imperfections that make us human. Our bond was not about perfection; it was about intention, about choosing to show up, again and again, for each other. And now, even in his absence, I carry forward the lessons he taught me—about love, forgiveness, and what it truly means to be a father and a son.

Reflecting on these moments now, I see how fragile life's threads can be and how easily everything could have unraveled. Yet, here we are—not defined by the scars but strengthened by them. Those scars, once symbols of hurt, have become badges of survival, proof that we have endured, healed, and grown.

Life has taught me that every day offers a choice. I could have nurtured bitterness or sorrow, allowing them to take root and consume me. Instead, I chose to seek joy and meaning. The memories of hardship became guideposts, pointing me toward kindness, love, and the ability to find light even in the darkest corners.

With every passing day, I cling to optimism, knowing that the strength we've built and the love we share will carry us through any storm. God's plan is unwavering, providing a foundation beneath every step forward. This journey's outcome is survival and triumph—a story of Oakland Hills and Milwaukee Rivers, of lessons learned and love reclaimed. It's the story of us, a narrative still being written, one day, one memory, one brush stroke at a time. My next journey isn't one of nostalgia but one with a different ending.

Looking back now, I realize that survival was never just about willpower. It wasn't merely grit, luck, or stubbornness that carried me forward when everything around me was crumbling. It was support—an invisible force stitched together by people who fought for me when I didn't even know I was in a battle. They loved me with a kind of love that didn't ask for recognition, didn't need applause, and didn't demand anything in return. Their sacrifices were made in silence, their prayers whispered in rooms I never entered, and their grace stretched farther than any of my mistakes could ever reach.

Some came momentarily, showing up in the exact season when their strength was needed. Others stayed longer, pouring into the cracks that threatened to undo me. But there was one... one who gave until there was nothing left to give; one who built bridges over waters too deep and too wild for me to cross alone; one who loved past my flaws, past my fears, past even my understanding of love itself.

OAKLAND HILLS, MILWAUKEE RIVERS

Aunt Grace.

She was more than family; she was the steady hand that kept trembling lives from falling apart. She was the intercessor whose prayers became the net that caught us when life tried to break us. She was the voice in the middle of the storm, the calm in the chaos, and the shield protecting us from dangers we were too young, broken, or blind to recognize. She was the living proof that sometimes the greatest battles are fought not with weapons, but with unwavering love and relentless faith.

And the truth is, her story is not just part of my story.

It is the foundation of it.

Without understanding her, you cannot fully understand me.

We sometimes tell the story of survival as if we stood alone on the battlefield, as if every wound was ours to bear and every victory to claim. But the truth is far more complicated—and far more beautiful.

My survival was never a solo act. It was the unseen prayers, the quiet sacrifices, and the open doors that someone else held long before I had the strength to walk through them.

And no one held that door longer or loved harder than Aunt Grace. Her hands steadied generations, and her faith caught us when nothing else would. She was more than a woman, more than a mother figure, and more than family. She was the grace that carried me when I couldn't hold myself. You'll meet her repeatedly—in memories, silence, resilience, and spaces where love refused to leave. Aunt Grace didn't just save me; she shaped me. Part III closed a door I had spent years knocking on—the longing for answers, for apologies, and for people to show up who never did. And though some pain still echoed in the quiet, something had shifted. I no longer needed every piece of the past to be explained. What I needed was something I hadn't yet learned to name: healing that didn't come from the source of the wound.

That's when Aunt Grace became more than a caretaker. She answered prayers I was too hurt to pray out loud. Her love didn't ask questions. It didn't take attendance. It simply arrived—and stayed. This next part of the story does not revisit broken places. It's where redemption begins. It's where silence gives way to covering. This is where grace and Mercie meet.

"Some call it mercy. I called her Auntie."

Grace & Mercie

"Some call it mercy. I called her Auntie."

They say grace is what covers you, and mercy is what keeps you. But I learned early on that both could come wrapped in the arms of a single woman.

Her name was Mercie, but we will call her Aunt Grace.

She wasn't just the woman who raised me; she was the quiet prayer I didn't know whispered in the chaos. She embodied discipline wrapped in tenderness and strength seasoned with stillness. She didn't always say much, but when she looked at you, it was as if she saw beyond your present and spoke to who you were becoming.

I chose to call this section *Grace & Mercie*, not just because of what she did—but because of who she was. She was the *mercy* that stepped in when life could've gone another way. She was the *grace* that reminded me I was still worthy of love, even when I didn't believe it for myself.

As you read these next chapters, know this: these are not just stories about a woman. These are stories about **redemption, rescue,** and **the kind of love that lifts even when it's tired.** This is where the healing began.

This is where destiny met the boy I was—and gave him room to grow into purpose.

CHAPTER 23
The Hidden Cost of Love

"People's sacrifices are often noticed only after we've already received the good from them. The things they gave up—their time, voice, strength—were all used to make life better, even if it wasn't for themselves."

Sometimes I don't think people really understood what she was to us. No, not just *who* she was, but *what* she meant. Aunt Grace wasn't just family—she was our fortress. She was the iron that refused to bend, the arms that never grew weary, the voice that sang lullabies into broken spirits and prayed over souls that had long stopped praying for themselves. She was our foundation. And she was stability. The kind that went unnoticed until it began to crack under the pressure of the very ones it held.

She was taken for granted.

I did it.
They did it.
We all did it.

But why?

Maybe for some of us, it was ignorance—too young or too distracted to understand the magnitude of who she was. But for others, it was a willful disregard, a quiet entitlement, as if she'd always be there. Aunt Grace had a heart of gold. But more than that—she was Heaven's steward, sent to intercept the devil's plans and reroute our family's future. She wasn't the stereotypical Black mom that society often tries to portray through flattened tropes. No. She was divinely assigned. An angel without wings, with gentle hands and a calming voice. She was a gift—anointed, chosen, and unshakeable.

Aunt Grace was the kind of gift you didn't recognize until you'd already broken the ribbon, torn the paper, and discarded the box—only to realize too late that what was inside… was everything.

* * *

I remember when I first came to deeply understand her power—when her name stopped being a title and became a testimony. I was living in Milwaukee, freshly uprooted from California, with my life in boxes and my identity trying to catch up. I moved into that house on the Northside with my cousins—five bedrooms packed with bodies and stories. The air always felt full—full of warmth, full of noise, full of life.

Aunt Grace's room was off to the right of the front door. The den. Not even a real bedroom. A makeshift space with an accordion door that folded like the gentle pages of a well-worn Bible. It didn't offer much in privacy. It creaked when you opened it, and never fully closed, but somehow that space became sacred. She could've claimed the biggest room in the house. But that wasn't her way. She chose humility every time. The matriarch didn't need a throne. She made her peace wherever she laid her head.

Each morning, she moved with rhythm and routine. Up before the sun, pressing her uniform, slipping into those white shoes that squeaked down the hallway. She worked in the cafeteria of a nearby elementary school, serving children with the same love and structure she gave us at home. You'd think she'd slow down. You'd think she'd put herself first for once.

But she didn't. She couldn't. Not with six more kids to raise—her grandchildren. All of them. Life had dealt some challenges with her children, and instead of watching the family scatter, Aunt Grace opened her arms—and her home. She refused to let the children be separated. And so, they came. One after the other. No questions asked. No complaints. Just love in action.

It wasn't a small feat. It was sacrifice. Daily. Quiet. Relentless. Unpaid. And we all knew it.

And then came I—another mouth, another need, another soul to tend to. And yet, she looked at me and said, "I'll love you like my own." And she meant it even though we weren't bound by blood.

You see, Aunt Grace was my aunt through marriage, not by blood, DNA, or any scientific thread that people use to validate a connection. My biological grandmother had married Aunt Grace's biological father. Because Aunt Grace was the oldest of them, they all formed bonds and truly became brothers and sisters despite having different parents.

But in the Black community, that's still family. Period.

Titles like "auntie," "cousin," "uncle," or "granny" aren't always traced through Ancestry.com. They're forged through moments—birthdays celebrated together, tears wiped without hesitation, meals shared in tight kitchens where laughter and greens simmered in the same pot. We love each other as family. And that love doesn't require a blood test.

But to outsiders looking in—those who didn't know the whole story, those who had the privilege of tracing lineage without complication—it wasn't always seen that way.

To them, it was a technicality.
To us, it was a testimony.

And that's what made it even more profound.

Because Aunt Grace didn't have to love me. She wasn't obligated. There was no court order. No legal agreement. No social worker pressing her to take me in. She chose to—*freely*. And in doing so, she modeled the kind of love that transcends paper trails and genetic ties.

She *opted* into a level of responsibility that most run from. Do you know what it means to take someone else's child into your home? To look into the face of a child whose life has been disrupted—who doesn't quite belong, doesn't quite fit, and is carrying the baggage of loss, confusion, or abandonment—and say, "You are mine now. I'll cover you. I'll feed you. I'll protect you. I'll love you like I birthed you."

That's what Aunt Grace did. And she did it with no complaints. Not one single one.

She became mother, auntie, counselor, and intercessor in one breath. That kind of love—the kind that isn't required but is *still* extended—is sacred. It's the kind of love that mirrors the heart of God.

And when people questioned it and asked why she'd do so much for someone who was not her "real" nephew, she didn't flinch. She didn't explain herself. She didn't need to. Because the love she gave wasn't up for debate. It was demonstrated.

And in a world where so many people love with conditions, Aunt Grace loved despite them.

She raised me without treating me like a favor. She folded me into the family quilt so seamlessly that most people didn't know there were stitches holding me in place, until jealousy or judgment pulled at the thread.

"You Ain't even real family."

That line... it echoed in moments of insecurity. Imagine being 2,000 miles away from your parents, feeling abandoned, unsure if you were wanted *anywhere*, and hearing those words in the one place you were supposed to feel safe.

On paper, maybe they were right. But in spirit, in experience, in the meals cooked, the rides to school, the prayers whispered over me while I slept—they were wrong.

OAKLAND HILLS, MILWAUKEE RIVERS

I was *real family*.

Because family isn't just blood. It's sacrifice. It's choice. It's covenant.

Aunt Grace chose me. And that choice wasn't some small act of kindness. It was a monumental declaration of love.

She looked past what separated us and leaned fully into what united us.

And that's what made it sacred. That's what made it *profound*.

Because to take on the responsibility of loving someone, that the world says you don't owe anything to—and doing it so well, so completely, so selflessly that no one can tell the difference—that's not just family.

That's legacy.

That's Aunt Grace.

* * *

One night, I was sitting on the porch. The crickets chirped in the distance, the wind rustled through the trees that lined the street, and the air held that Midwest humidity that made your shirt stick to your back. The porch was my thinking place. And just beside it was Aunt Grace's picture window—her view into the world. That window faced the gas station where we'd run errands, grab late-night snacks, or pick up her favorite drink.

Pepsi.

But not just any Pepsi. It had to be in a bottle. And she poured salted peanuts right into it for reasons I didn't understand. The carbonation bubbled around the nuts like a science experiment, and she'd drink it like it was the best thing on Earth. I had never seen that before. Maybe it was a Milwaukee thing, or perhaps it was an Aunt Grace thing. Either way, it was *her* thing.

From her window, she knocked. "Key Key, come here, honey."

"Yes, ma'am!" I replied, jumping up. One of the earliest lessons she taught me: "Yes ma'am, no ma'am, yes sir, no sir." Respect wasn't negotiable—it was the law. If you forgot, her eyes would correct you before her mouth ever did. And if you were slow to fix it, you'd get that "alright now," which meant you were on thin ice.

I ran inside. She sat by the phone, its long, stretched-out cord dangling like a lifeline. "It's your mom," she said, handing me the receiver.

I hadn't heard her voice in a while. We spoke briefly about how I was doing, what I'd eaten, and whether I was adjusting. She said she missed me. I said I missed her, too. But we both knew it was better for me to be where I was. With *Aunt Grace*.

When the call ended, my mother asked to speak with Aunt Grace. I handed over the phone and stepped back as they talked. I didn't catch everything, but I could tell the conversation included money, promises, and maybe a few regrets. Raising a growing boy wasn't cheap, especially with a never-ending appetite. But Aunt Grace never shared that it was a burden because love,to her, never kept score.

* * *

I shared a room with Jamal. Our room was upstairs, on the left side of the hallway. Across from us were our other cousins. Down the hall, near the bathroom, was Veronica, who needed her space to raise her little boy.

It wasn't much, but it was ours. In the room Jamal and I shared, we had two twin beds on opposite sides, and a short wooden dresser stood between them. One drawer each, sometimes two if the season changed and we needed to squeeze in winter clothes. The wood was scratched up from years of use, the handles were mismatched, and the top always had at least one loose quarter or a pair of broken headphones. That dresser told its own story—of growing boys, hand-me-downs, and childhood stretching itself inside small spaces.

The room also had a small closet—and I mean small. It was barely deep enough to hold more than a few hangers or a couple of neatly folded outfits stacked in a milk crate on the floor. But we made it work. You learn quickly in a house like that, packed with people, love, and noise, how to make the most of every inch.

OAKLAND HILLS, MILWAUKEE RIVERS

What made the room special, though—what made it *ours*—was the window.

Just beneath it was the roof covering the front porch—a flat stretch of shingles that we treated like our private balcony. On summer nights or lazy afternoons, Jamal and I would pop open that old window and climb out like we were sneaking into another world. We'd sit there, enjoying the cool breeze brushing against our skin as we looked over the block. Sometimes we'd yell at our cousins riding their bikes or walking to the corner store. Other times, we'd shout down to our friends, laughing about whatever happened at school or daring them to race to the stop sign and back. We'd stay out there, soaking up the moment, until we heard the infamous signal:

"Oooh, Granny, they're on that roof again," one of our cousins would shout.

That was our cue to climb back inside quickly before Granny came with that look that meant *business*.

That rooftop wasn't just shingles and slope. It was our skybox to the world. Our vantage point on life unfolding in the neighborhood.

And here's the thing—I would have *never* had that experience living in Oakland.

In Oakland, everything felt tighter, more rigid. You didn't just climb out of windows and sit on rooftops. You didn't yell at kids from above or wave at neighbors who waved back. Life there was busier. Faster. Edgier. There were no porches like that, no freedom to explore a block where everybody knew your name. In Oakland, you looked over your shoulder. At least on that porch roof, I could look ahead in Milwaukee.

That room, that house, that roof—it gave me a different kind of childhood. One that wasn't shaped by flashy things or wide-open spaces, but by togetherness. By the sound of cousins arguing over who ate the last snack. By the smell of grease from Sunday dinner drifting up through the vents. By the simple joy of sitting next to your cousin on a rooftop, believing for that moment that you were on top of the world.

It influenced how I saw family and community. For the first time in a long time, it made me feel like I belonged to something—like I was woven into the fabric of a family, not just a visitor in someone else's home.

But Aunt Grace's love wasn't just familial—it was sacred. What she gave wasn't born out of obligation or tradition, but out of a quiet knowing that she had been called to this. She didn't just open her home; she opened her heart with the certainty that she was fulfilling something greater than herself. And in doing so, she became more than a caretaker—she became a divine covering, stitched together by prayer, patience, and purpose.

Aunt Grace saw to that. And though the walls groaned under the weight of so many lives, she never stopped opening doors for more. That's what matriarchs do: they cover you when you don't realize it's raining.

CHAPTER 24
Divine Covering

"Protection comes in many forms: a conversation, an act, or a prayer. It all serves a purpose to cover something that is deemed to have value and add to life."

Every Sunday, church was non-negotiable. It wasn't up for discussion. It wasn't up for debate or dependent on how you felt when you woke up. It was expected—etched into the rhythm of our week like breath and breakfast. Four blocks away, just a short walk from the house. But if you weren't ready when that van was pulling out of the driveway? You walked. Simple as that.

And Aunt Grace was never late. Not once.

She was faithful to Sunday School. Faithful like clockwork. She didn't just attend—she *taught*. Some weeks, she'd be up late on Saturday night, surrounded by her lesson books and that well-worn Bible with tissue-soft pages. You'd hear the faint sound of her humming gospel music, the scratch of her pen highlighting scriptures, and her whispering softly as she prepared her lesson. She was always ready. Always in position. And if we weren't, that was on us.

DIVINE COVERING

She never nagged us to hurry. On Sundays, we'd get the occasional shout up the stairs: "Y'all hurry up! I'm getting ready to leave." If we weren't ready after that warning, she'd leave. Gracefully. Without fuss. And we knew exactly what that meant. If you got left behind, you better lace up your shoes and make that walk. Because Aunt Grace didn't play when it came to God. You respected the house of the Lord and her commitment to it.

But going to church wasn't just a spiritual act. For us, it was a full-body experience—mental, emotional, and even physical. Church services were *long*. Some Sundays felt like marathons. You had to sit still, pay attention, and keep your attitude in check. Disrespecting the service—by talking too much, playing, or dozing off—was not tolerated. Aunt Grace had that look, that subtle turn of the head from her seat, that would reset your whole posture.

And snacks were survival.

Church meant "in-between service" money—those precious 30 minutes between Sunday School and morning service when we could run to the corner store. But not with regular cash. No, what we had were *food stamps*. The old kind. Not a card or a digital swipe. These came in a thick paper booklet, with bills in different colors—$1s, $5s, $10s—all textured and stiff. You tore them out like raffle tickets. For some, it was a mark of poverty. For us, it was a passport to joy.

We weren't ashamed. Everybody we knew had them. My mom had them in California, and my Aunt Grace had them in Milwaukee. They were part of inner-city life—how families like ours survived. For us kids, food stamps meant hot chips, a Little Debbie cake, or maybe a Faygo soda before sitting through a three-hour service. That one snack had to last, because once service started, that was it.

Aunt Grace made sure we had it. Even when money was tight and mouths were many, she found a way. That was the miracle of her life—how she stretched the little she had to care for so many. We didn't always understand it back then. We just thought she *had* it. But now? As an adult, I realize she didn't. What she had was *faith*. And God made the rest happen.

She knew how to budget. How to prioritize. How to share. How to make sure every child in that house—and even some that weren't—had something to eat, wear, and a chance to feel joy. She didn't hoard her resources. She multiplied them. Food stamps didn't embarrass her. They were a tool. And in her hands, they became a ministry.

After church, we'd all pile into the big blue van. That van was a legend—an aging beast that squeaked down the street, loaded with kids in church clothes and the lingering scent of peppermint and hair grease. If there weren't a second service, we'd head straight home. But if there was one, we knew what that meant—food.

And not just any food.

Down in the basement fellowship hall, the kitchen committee laid out a spread like it was Thanksgiving every Sunday: fried chicken that cracked when you bit into it, mac and cheese so creamy it slid off the spoon, collard greens with ham hocks, cornbread, banana pudding, and punch to wash it all down.

But that Sunday, we didn't stay. There was no afternoon service, no second sermon, no post-service meal. This time, we went home.

Still, the spirit lingered.

Aunt Grace sat in the front seat, humming a hymn under her breath, with her Bible resting on the dashboard. And as the van bumped along the street, I looked out the window and thought about how blessed we really were, not because we had a lot, but because we had *her*.

That Sunday, like every Sunday, wasn't just about church. It was about family. It was about structure. It was about survival. And Aunt Grace was the bridge that connected all three.

Little did I know then that her faith carried us through things we didn't even realize we were facing.

* * *

DIVINE COVERING

Church was never just about attending service—it was about aligning with God, family, and the rhythm of life in our household. Aunt Grace was the center of that alignment. Her walk with God was steady, sincere, and undeniable. It bled through everything she did—how she spoke, how she carried herself, and how she loved us.

We didn't just *go* to church because it was expected—we went because she *led* us there. Week after week. Her faith wasn't loud or boastful. It moved through her like breath—quiet, steady, and always present. You could see it in her eyes when she'd whisper a prayer over dinner. You could feel it in the softness of her voice when she said, "Thank you, Lord," even on the hardest days. It was in her Bible that stayed within reach—on the nightstand, the couch, the kitchen counter. God wasn't just someone she worshiped on Sunday. He lived in that house with us, because Aunt Grace made room for Him.

And in that space, something beautiful happened between her and me.

Our relationship was special—rooted in a shared reverence for God, but also her trust in me. There weren't many in the house who shared in those spiritual conversations. Aunt Grace's children, while loving and connected to her, didn't always engage in that way. Most of them avoided church unless it was a special occasion—Mother's Day, Family & Friends Day, or an event where food was involved and she needed help with something. But I showed up. And not because I had to, but because something in me *wanted* to.

There was a bond we formed through those quiet Saturday nights when I'd pass her room and see her preparing her Sunday School lesson. She'd look up and ask, "Y'all studying this same lesson tomorrow?" Sometimes I'd say "yes, ma'am," sometimes "no, ma'am." Either way, I'd be invited to sit, to listen, to learn. It wasn't a formal Bible study. It was spiritual storytelling. And it was *ours*.

So, when I made the decision to leave Aunt Grace's church and join another congregation, it wasn't something I took lightly. I was only 14, but I felt the shift in my spirit—the desire to grow in a different direction. There was a young pastor from Aunt Grace's church who had recently launched his own in the city. His style was fresh, his sermons relevant, and his passion undeniable. He spoke in a way that resonated with my generation in a relatable way.

I remember walking into Aunt Grace's room one evening and saying, "Auntie, I think I want to join Pastor Lamont's church."

She looked at me, paused for a moment, and then, without hesitation, said, "Okay, baby."

That was it. No guilt trip. No questioning my loyalty. Just trust. She trusted my judgment, trusted the God in me, and maybe, more than anything, she trusted that the seeds she had planted would continue to grow—even in different soil.

I still lived in her house. Still ate at her table. Still said "yes ma'am" when she called. But spiritually, I had begun a new journey. And the most remarkable thing? She never made me feel like I had to choose between her love and my spiritual path. That kind of grace is rare.

During this transition, something else unfolded in the background—quiet but worth noting.

One of my older cousins, who still lived in the house with us at the time, had started dating Pastor Lamont. For a season, she too became active in the church. She was there every Sunday, sitting up front, helping out where needed. There was a buzz in the air—people whispering, wondering if she'd become the First Lady.

But here's the thing: being a First Lady in the Black church isn't just about sitting on the front row in a fancy hat. It's a calling. A weight. A responsibility that extends beyond Sunday service. First Ladies are often expected to lead the women's ministry, mentor young girls, organize fundraisers, be a counselor, a model wife, a spiritual support, and still hold her own smile when life is unraveling behind closed doors. It's a ministry all its own. And not everyone wants that role.

My cousin didn't. She liked the *man*, but not the mantle that came with him. And when the relationship ended, so did her membership. Her exit was quiet, graceful, and unannounced. No farewell speech. Just a slow drift away from the pew.

But I remained. Because my decision wasn't tied to a relationship, it was tied to revelation. Something had awakened in me, and I needed to see where it led.

Even while living under Aunt Grace's roof, I charted my own course spiritually, and she never once made me feel like I had betrayed her. If anything, I think she admired my decision. It reminded her of herself. That quiet boldness. That sense of calling. That unshakable faith.

In the years that followed, we continued to share sacred moments. Conversations about scripture. Reflections on sermons. Late-night talks about how God moves through the lives of people. It wasn't something she shared with everyone. In fact, I realized just how rare it was—how few had that kind of closeness with her. Not because she was distant. But because not everyone was open to what she had to give spiritually.

Our bond was anchored in trust. She trusted that I would honor God in whatever church I attended. And I trusted her to keep covering me in prayer no matter where I went.

That's what made it so profound.

She didn't need me to be in her church to still be in her heart.

And as the house around us continued to fill and shift and stretch to hold more lives, our relationship remained steady. In the midst of transitions—spiritually, emotionally, and logistically—she never lost sight of me. And I never lost sight of her. She remained my anchor.

What made it even more powerful was how rare that relationship was. Many of my cousins often felt like Aunt Grace was trying to convert them or guilt them back into church. And truthfully, she *was*. But not in a loud or forceful way. She didn't believe in beating people over the head with the Bible. She simply had a quiet, persistent way of nudging people toward God. Her voice was soft. Her spirit was settled. And every so often, you'd hear her say something like, "You need to make God the head of your life."

OAKLAND HILLS, MILWAUKEE RIVERS

That was it. No long lecture. No heated debates. Just a simple, soul-cutting statement wrapped in maternal grace.

They'd nod, half-listening, and go on with their day. But I always believed something stuck. Because Aunt Grace's words had a way of planting themselves in the heart, even when people didn't realize they were growing roots. Her desire was never hidden—she wanted her family to be saved. She wanted each of us to know God for ourselves and walk with Him like she did. That wasn't a secret. It was her heart's cry. She was a living witness of what it meant to be carried by grace, and I… I was becoming one, too.

It's moments like that I often go back to—especially now, when I think about everything she carried, everything she poured, and everything she was to us.

To me.

Because when you're raised by a woman like Aunt Grace, you don't just remember her.

You become shaped by her.

And that shaping? That spiritual legacy?

It never fades.

What's always been fascinating is how multi-layered she was. You couldn't define Aunt Grace in a single sentence. She was complex in the best way. She was the protector—shielding us from the storms life tried to throw our way. She was the lover of God—unapologetic in her devotion, yet patient with those who weren't there yet. She was the problem solver—quietly putting pieces back together when things fell apart. She was, in so many ways, the savior—not in the divine sense, but in the practical. The one who stepped in when others stepped out. The one who said "yes" when life gave everyone else a reason to say "no."

But most importantly—she was the fisherman.

That title and role meant more than just casting a rod into a lake.

DIVINE COVERING

Fishing was her sanctuary. It was her escape. It was how she managed the weight of her world. When you carry as much as she did—raising children who weren't her own, holding a family together with love and duct tape, praying over souls while cooking Sunday dinner—*you need a release*. You need something that doesn't ask anything of you, but gives everything in return.

And for Aunt Grace, fishing was that place.

CHAPTER 25

Lakes, Rivers, and Streams

"Some life lessons cannot be taught by words alone. They must be learned through experience and time."

You know, water has always meant something deep to me—something I didn't always know how to explain. Being born in California is what initially connected me to it. The tranquility of its presence. The way it moves without force, yet can shape the world around it. It holds this quiet power—an authority that doesn't need to raise its voice. And when I came to Milwaukee, I discovered that power in a new way. It became more than a metaphor. It became a vehicle to gather memories, all in one activity – fishing. And, Aunt Grace is the reason for it.

The way she introduced me to fishing was different. It wasn't just about being on the water—it was about discovering refuge. A place where people escaped, not to run from life, but to find themselves within it. And for those lucky enough to be in her life, she made sure we learned how to cast a line—not just into the water, but into something deeper. Into experience.

Those experiences taught us lessons you couldn't always get in a classroom: patience, competition, and survival, because you couldn't go fishing without

LAKES, RIVERS, AND STREAMS

having at least one day when you got skunked. A day when the fish weren't biting. The cows could be standing up. You could be holding your mouth just right. You could have every kind of bait in the tackle box.

Still, there'd be that one moment when nothing worked. You wouldn't catch a fish.

Unless you were Aunt Grace.

She had a way with fishing—somehow, she always brought something back. It was her quiet gift, which felt more like communion than a sport.

It was like the fish were showing their appreciation for her spirit, her peace, her presence.

But the truth is, for the rest of us, not catching anything was okay. Because even without a fish in your bucket, it was always better to be on the water with Aunt Grace.

Fishing was a cornerstone in Aunt Grace's life—a ritual, an escape, a reset button. It was her therapy. I believe it was the one space where she could breathe without expectations, where she wasn't someone's problem solver, not a caretaker, not "Granny, Ma, Auntie," or the fierce matriarch. She was just Aunt Grace, anchored to her own peace.

Every weekday, she worked at the elementary school near the house, serving lunch to the neighborhood kids. You knew when your favorites were on the menu—mock chicken legs, pizza, or blueberry cobbler—because she'd bring home extras wrapped up just for us. You could always count on the smell of school food mixing with the scent of fried fish or cornbread in the house. She wore that classic all-white cafeteria uniform—apron tied tight around her waist, a hairnet over her curls, and a loving scowl that kept kids in line and adults in check.

Aunt Grace took care of everyone. That's who she was. Her house was never empty—a revolving door of folks who needed a place to stay, a hot plate, a few dollars, or someone to listen. She gave freely, without complaint. Yet, people often took advantage of that kindness. I saw it. The ones who never brought anything to the table drained her time, stole her money, or tried to break her spirit—they always found a way back or around. Still, she smiled. Still, she gave. She'd say, "God blessed me to be a blessing." I believe my compassion and sense of duty to others were rooted right there, as I watched Aunt Grace choose grace even when people didn't deserve it. I would observe her and sit in amazement. How could someone working part-time be blessed with cars, houses, and money to support multiple people? Especially when she didn't have to. I recognized that her heart was always focused on blessing others, and I believe that's why God favored her so much.

But when she wasn't being everybody's rock, she was on the water. That was her sanctuary. Her big blue van—stained seats, snack wrappers on the dash, tackle boxes and 50-gallon coolers piled in the back—was our vessel to freedom. One of her favorite places was Wind Lake, about 45 minutes south of Milwaukee. The lake wasn't in the city but tucked off a quiet road in Racine County. You could see it from the highway, shining like glass, with the houses perched perfectly along its rim like guardians. But Wind Lake didn't welcome just anyone. You needed a boat. No shore fishing allowed. Without one, you were trespassing. And, the town's property owners or police had no problem letting you know of it.

Of course, Aunt Grace came prepared. She had two boats. One was a beat-up 14-foot flat-bottom aluminum boat that we called "Casanova." My favorite. It was old and rugged, like a pair of hands that had done a lot of work and pulled by an old rusty trailer. The trailer was wrapped in old, salvaged carpet to ensure enough protection from the two metals touching. We'd sometimes have to replace the old grey masking tape that held it tightly on the trailer. We attempted to prevent additional damage to the boat. One of the rivets under the seat had a slow leak, and by the time we got halfway across the lake, a thin puddle would form in the back. We used an old piece of a couch cushion to soak it up. Often, after I rowed us across the lake, I'd be in charge of wringing it out every 15 minutes—my way of feeling helpful, part of something.

The other boat was a four-seater motorboat from the '70s, painted in a strange shade of seafoam green with off-white trim. The boy cousins loved it. No rowing. We could fly across the water like kings. The seats were worn and soft, like the family couch you can't throw away. When it got cold or the younger kids became sleepy, they'd crawl under the bow with blankets and curl up like little sardines.

One particular evening stands out. There were four carloads of us that evening. We caravanned down to Wind Lake, laughing and hollering out of windows, coolers packed with snacks from Aldi, and rods rattling in the trunks. We rented extra boats from the old man whose house sat at the bend of the road. You had to rent if you didn't bring your own—Wind Lake ensured that.

We always tried to get on the water before sunset. Aunt Grace had a specific spot—a secret marked by the tallest tree on a nearby island and a house light across the lake. "Row up a little more. You see that tallest tree? Line up with that light from the house," she'd say, calm but commanding. And when the boat aligned, she'd sit back like a queen reclaiming her throne. She always found the fish. Always.

That night, the fish seemed to be biting slower than usual. We only had a few in the boat and were waiting patiently for a new school of them to come through. While we all were sitting there—all four boats—the air began to cool. The warm day met the chill of night, and suddenly a mist formed. Not a fog—a mist. Light, thin, and low, like something out of a horror movie where shadows creep between the trees. The lake was so still it looked painted. The moon lit the surface in silver, and the mist danced above it, ghostlike and elegant. It felt like time had paused.

We all had our lines dropped while waiting. The crappies hadn't returned with their second round of biting yet. When fish didn't bite, you couldn't go back to shore. That was the rule. You had to wait it out. We passed the time watching the minnows circling the lantern light, which hung over the side of the boat from our oars, darting like synchronized swimmers. Some of us told quiet jokes, hypothesized about the fish being asleep, or snacked on chips and candy we had tucked away in a grocery bag. Others just leaned back and gazed at the stars.

Then came the croaking.

OAKLAND HILLS, MILWAUKEE RIVERS

From the island nestled not too far from the shore where we launched our boats, a chorus of frogs began their midnight song. Deep, rhythmic croaks layered and echoed. It felt like the lake itself was humming. It wasn't just background noise—it was a soundtrack. And we sat still, quiet, listening.

Roscoe was on the water with us that night. He was in another boat about 30 feet away with some other folks. He was a family friend, one of Aunt Grace's favorites. He had that deep Southern drawl, thick like syrup, and a voice that cracked with wisdom and old jokes. Then we noticed something interesting. For some reason, the frogs stopped croaking, the family stopped talking, and the wind stopped blowing. We were in pure silence. And after an hour, Roscoe broke out and said, "It's so quiet out here, you can hear a rat lick lard."

For a few seconds, no one said a word. I guess we were all still processing it. Then it hit us. One by one, boats full of cousins, friends, and family erupted in laughter. The sound carried across the water like music. We laughed so hard we had to reel in our lines. I remember Aunt Grace wiping tears from her eyes, shaking her head at Roscoe, her gold teeth flickering in the lantern light. It was an epic moment.

The night wore on, and we kept fishing, the quiet settling in once more—only interrupted by the gentle lapping of water against the sides of the boat as darkness wrapped around us. Then, without warning, Aunt Grace would burst into laughter—one of those high-pitched, joyful, full-bodied laughs that bubbled up from deep in her belly and danced across the lake. It was hearty and contagious, the kind of laugh that made you join in even if you didn't know what was funny.

In that moment, reflecting once more on what Roscoe had said, her laughter ignited a spark in us, triggering a chain reaction of giggles and chuckles that spread across the water like ripples from a stone. And somehow, it felt as if it continued indefinitely.

Those were the kinds of nights Aunt Grace gave us.

And then there was the Big Green Lake.

LAKES, RIVERS, AND STREAMS

That trip was different. It was another weekend, another mission. Aunt Grace had heard rumors of bluegills and catfish biting strongly up near Highway 23. It was not uncommon for us to spend a weekend fishing and visiting different spots to fill up our cooler. This was no different. We loaded the blue van with coolers, gear, and all the kids. Her best friend, Janice, came, too, along with Joe.

We started early and tried a few lakes first. The bites were slow after fishing all night and most of the day. Aunt Grace wasn't satisfied. She didn't believe in coming home empty-handed. Then, at one lake, a fisherman tipped her off to where the fish were biting: Big Green Lake. The biggest, deepest inland lake in Wisconsin. Home to every freshwater fish imaginable.

We made it there just before dusk. The spot we chose had a narrow channel near County Road A, perfect for catching catfish at night and bluegills in the morning. We set up our gear—tightline poles, bobbers, nightcrawlers, and folding chairs—and waited. That night, the catfish came fast and steady. Rods were bending every few minutes. Aunt Grace's eyes lit up every time a fish hit the line.

And it was her joy—you could hear it in her laugh as she got bite after bite. That laugh—high-pitched, unfiltered, and bursting with excitement—rose from deep in her belly and spilled into the air like sunlight breaking through clouds. Every chuckle was a celebration; every shout of "I got another one!" came with a rhythm that matched the heartbeat of the lake. She'd lean back in her chair, gripping her rod with both hands, and giggle like a little girl as she reeled them in. You'd see her rocking with laughter, her whole body moving, and the dirt shifting slightly beneath her feet as she set the hook. Even the fish seemed to dance at the end of her line, as if they too were part of the joy. It was more than just catching fish—it was witnessing Aunt Grace fully in her element, fully alive. In those moments, the worries of the world faded. Time stood still, and all that remained was the sound of water, the tug of a line, and the beautiful sound of her joy echoing across the lake.

By morning, the sun crept over the trees, casting a golden shimmer on the channel. It was a warm Sunday, the sun was steady at a comfortable 75 degrees, and it was the kind of day where even the breeze felt like a blessing.

OAKLAND HILLS, MILWAUKEE RIVERS

The bluegills showed up big and bold, each a slab worthy of bragging rights. We started filling the cooler quickly. However, we knew our time was ending soon. You see, Aunt Grace was a devout, loyal, unshakeable Christian, and she made sure that when fishing, we left early in the morning so she could get back to church. It was her routine. It was her standard. It was her way. As the time progressed, Aunt Grace said something I never thought I'd hear: "We're not going to church. I'm staying here to fish."

The silence that followed was thick. We all paused, unsure if we heard her right. But the fish were biting, and nobody questioned her.

Later that morning, the fish slowed down biting, so we moved to another side of the lake. Just me, Aunt Grace, and Janice. She set up two poles—one with a bobber, one on the bottom. Aunt Grace started catching a few fish, but it was nothing to brag about. She tossed a few four or five-inch bluegills in the bucket next to her. The pole she had on the bottom rested on a rock on the bank. She'd pay attention to it while fishing for bluegills. It was at that moment when the thump came. A bite. Her rod jerked hard. "Oooh, that's a big one!" she shouted. She grabbed her rod, quickly set the hook, and started reeling it, expecting a catfish. But as it broke the surface, it wasn't a fish. It was a mudpuppy.

"AAAAAAH!" she screamed, throwing the pole down and bolting back toward the van. "That's the devil!" she hollered.

We looked at the slimy, grey creature with its red, fanned gills. It was alien and prehistoric—like something pulled from a nightmare. We carefully unhooked it and let it go, but Aunt Grace was convinced that was God's punishment for fishing on a Sunday.

She never did it again.

That moment stuck with me—not just because of the scream or the mystery of the mudpuppy, but because it reminded me of who Aunt Grace was. She was a woman of principle. Even in joy, she had lines she wouldn't cross. It was a lesson I never forgot: If you have a standard, keep it. No moment of pleasure is worth the regret that might follow. Aunt Grace taught us that, on the water, in the kitchen, and in every quiet, sacrificial way she lived her life.

Fishing wasn't just a way to catch dinner; it was a way to remember, a way to gather, and a way to teach. Through it, Aunt Grace gave us all more than full freezers—she gave us peace, legacy, and stories that would carry on long after the water stilled.

These moments were reasons why I loved her so much. The opportunities she provided and the lessons she taught helped to define me as a person. And, it didn't stop during fishing trips, but expanded even more at home. She nurtured and taught me to be the best version of myself, to create options to reduce the need to struggle like she did.

But what Aunt Grace gave me extended far beyond fish fries and quiet lessons on the lake. She allowed me to grow, dream, and, eventually, be honest about who I was. Her love wasn't loud, but it was unwavering, and it wrapped around me like a quilt passed down through generations: warm, weighted, and stitched with sacrifice. As I began to face the parts of myself that felt hardest to share—with her, with my mother, and with the church—I held tightly to the one thing she had always offered without condition: safety. I would soon learn that kind of love doesn't just protect you; it prepares you for situations that may melt your heart and others that may break your soul.

CHAPTER 26
Unconditional Love

"Love has many powers, but the greatest is when it covers you."

Pleasing Aunt Grace was never a duty—it was a devotion. It was stitched into the rhythm of my life, like the beat of a heart you don't have to think about to feel. Birthdays, Mother's Days, Christmases... they were opportunities. Opportunities to flood her with gratitude could never match all she had poured into me. From shopping at Younkers, Boston Store, and Macy's, picking out the latest fashions carefully, to carrying pieces of the load so her shoulders didn't bear the full weight alone—everything I did was a whisper back to her: *I see you. I love you.*

Over time, we didn't just grow close because we shared holidays or traditions. We grew close because life demanded it, and our hearts accepted the call. Spiritually, we connected. Physically, we helped each other. But emotionally, that was where our roots ran deepest. She was my rock, and I regarded that relationship as seriously as breathing.

A certain kind of wonder comes with knowing you're loved unconditionally. To stand in front of someone, flaws and all, and still be seen as worthy—it's a kind of magic not everyone gets to experience. But with Aunt Grace, that wonder was my reality. She chose to love me; she didn't have to, and knowing that made her love extraordinary.

Growing up in the late 1990s and early 2000s, I learned that my pen could express things my mouth was too afraid to. Writing became my shelter, my sanctuary—a place where I could peel back the layers of who I was without fear. To take tangled emotions and messy thoughts, and place them neatly into words was a gift—and one I desperately needed for the moment that would soon come.

I spent my teenage years in Milwaukee, raised under the heavy blanket of spiritual discipline and religious tradition. But that blanket didn't always comfort—it sometimes suffocated. I remember the sermons: the thunderous voices from the pulpit, the way they carved judgments into the air with their words. Have you ever sat in a Black church and felt the preacher tear apart the core of who you are, all under the guise of righteousness? Felt the sting of your humanity reduced to a "sin," no matter the goodness you carried or the love you showed? That kind of rejection can lodge itself deep into your bones.

Each time they condemned those "living in sin," my heart clenched tighter. Behind my smiles, behind my good grades and service, I was hiding. I was battling something inside—a part of me I hadn't asked for or chosen, but which was as real as my heartbeat. I found women to be beautiful, and I even had girlfriends, but there was another attraction I couldn't shake: an attraction to men. Every time the sermons slammed down on that part of me, I wondered: Was I broken? Was I cursed?

Silent shadows whispered louder inside my mind. Was this who I was because of my past? Or was it something deeper, something woven into the fabric of me? Either way, the shame threatened to drown me. There were nights I wondered if it was even worth it—worth living, breathing, and carrying this secret. Because rejection cuts deeper than any physical wound. It tears at the soul.

And hovering over it all was Aunt Grace. *What would she say?* Would she look at me the same way if she knew the whole truth? Would the love that had been my anchor suddenly drift away?

You know, they say mothers have a sixth sense about their children. I always wondered if Aunt Grace had it, too. Part of me hoped she already knew that maybe she had been loving that hidden part of me all along. But I needed her to *know*. I needed her to *fully and completely see me* and still choose me.

So, I chose the only way I knew how to tell her: I wrote her a letter.

OAKLAND HILLS, MILWAUKEE RIVERS

Whoever said words were just letters on a page never knew the power a letter could hold. Mine carried my soul between its lines. I was no longer the teenager under her roof. I was grown, working, and living on my own. Yet the part of me that mattered most still longed for her approval and covering.

I sat in my room that day, my heart racing and hands shaking. With paper in front of me and pen hovering, I forced myself to write the words:

"I wanted you to know something intimate about me. A part of me I've been wanting to share with you for some time now, but was afraid to tell you. I love you so much, but I feel it's time you knew. I'm attracted to guys."

Writing those words felt like pulling a secret from my chest, laying it bare. I folded the letter neatly, my heart pounding, and drove to Aunt Grace's house. She wasn't home. Maybe she was shopping, or perhaps God knew I needed the courage without her eyes on me. Either way, I left it there—on her dresser—a confession left to the universe.

Days passed. Anxiety gnawed at me. Had she read it? Was she angry? Disappointed? Hurt?

Then the phone rang. I saw her name on the caller ID, and the ground beneath me seemed to sway.

I picked up. "Hello?"

"Hey, baby," she said, her voice like balm to a wounded heart. "I got your letter. I read it. And I want you to know that I love you, which will never change."

Tears pooled in my eyes.

"I already knew," she continued softly. "But I'm glad you trusted me enough to tell me. I love you even more for that."

The weight lifted. The sky opened. For the first time, I could breathe fully.

But peace has a peculiar way of being short-lived.

Somehow, that letter ended up in the hands of one of my cousins. And like wildfire, the news spread. My secret was no longer mine—it had become a family headline.

So, I did what few would have dared: I called for a family meeting.

Sitting in a room with 10 to 15 relatives, my heart thumping, I laid it bare.

"I wrote a letter to Aunt Grace," I began, voice steady. "It shared my sexual preferences. I'm standing on who I am. I'm not ashamed. Does anyone have a problem with this?"

One of my oldest cousins smiled and laughed, "We knew already. You didn't have to call a meeting for this, dude."

The room erupted into laughter. Hugs were shared. And life—blessedly—moved forward.

Aunt Grace's curiosity bloomed afterwards—tender, alive, and reaching for understanding like vines stretching toward the sun.
It would have been easy, even understandable, for her to tuck the conversation away in a quiet box labeled "things we don't talk about."
But she didn't.

Instead, she leaned in. She asked questions—simple ones at first—about my world, about the life I lived outside the family gatherings and Sunday dinners. Questions about the community I was a part of, about how same-sex relationships worked, and about what it meant to live openly and love fully when so much of the world still whispered behind closed doors.

There was no judgment in her tone and no hesitancy in her eyes. Only wonder remained. Only the kind of love that refuses to settle for silence when connection is still possible. Through those conversations—awkward sometimes, beautiful always—our bond didn't just survive; it deepened.

But Aunt Grace's curiosity wasn't the only one sparked; the ripple spread wider. Some of my cousins, who had once treated topics like sexuality as if they were forbidden territory, suddenly found themselves... wondering, searching, and trying.

I remember overhearing them talk about shows like Noah's Arc—a series that, for many of us, felt like a rare window into the stories of Black gay men living, loving, stumbling, and finding themselves unapologetically.

They laughed at the funny moments and paused at the tender ones. They watched, discussed, and watched again, trying to piece together a world they had never had to understand before.

In those moments, I found myself caught between gratitude and caution. I was grateful that they were trying, but I was cautious, wondering: Was this for me, or was it just curiosity?

There's a fragile space between being supported and being studied. Between someone seeking to understand you because they love you, and someone peering into your life like a visitor at a museum: intrigued but detached. I didn't always know which side of the line their interest fell on.

After all, I wasn't the villain that the media often portrayed. I didn't fit the exaggerated mold—the loud, flamboyant stereotype that people sometimes expect when they hear the word "gay." I was just me: a straight-acting man who laughed at bad jokes, loved hard, worked harder, and wore his Timberlands until the soles wore thin.

There were moments I wondered if they were disappointed not to find something more "interesting" to gossip about; moments when I questioned whether their curiosity came with strings—expectations I would never quite meet. And yet, even with all the silent questions floating in the air, one truth remained:

They showed up.
They asked questions.
They tried.

And perhaps love isn't always clean or perfect. Sometimes, love appears as messy conversations, uncomfortable silences, and family members awkwardly binge-watching Noah's Arc as they grasp for a glimpse into your world.

Aunt Grace stood at the center, steady as ever through it all. She didn't need to binge-watch anything. She didn't need to understand every term or concept; she understood me. That was enough.

Our bond, once built on family ties and childhood memories, was now strengthened by trust—by the willingness to step into uncharted waters together, hand in hand. She didn't let her lack of knowledge scare her away from what she did know: that I was hers. And that love—real, unconditional love—never asks you to hide.

And that understanding of that sacred, quiet, undeniable covering was everything I didn't even know I needed.

* * *

My mom had come to visit.

It was a milestone moment—one of those once-in-a-lifetime seasons where you feel overwhelmed and humbled by how far you've come. I was preparing for my doctoral graduation. Years of sacrifice, late nights, and prayers whispered into the darkness culminated in this moment.

My mother was staying with me in Madison, a small apartment that had witnessed the grind and the growth.

Our relationship had not always been smooth. There were seasons of distance, misunderstanding, and silence so loud it filled the space between us like fog. But this visit felt different. Healing had been quietly weaving its thread through our conversations, stitching us closer with each shared story and each word of grace.

In the days leading up to graduation, laughter filled the air. The easy kind—the kind that doesn't have to fight through bitterness or pain first.

It felt... good.
It felt earned.

One evening, we drove down to Milwaukee. The car was filled with a gentle quiet—the soft hum of the engine, the faint music playing from the radio, and the streetlights stretching into golden blurs as we moved forward. We had chatted lightly about food, the ceremony, and all the "typical mom things" she loved to bring up.

"So," she said with a playful tone, "when are you going to give me a grandchild?" I laughed it off, steering the car, offering vague answers, dodging the deeper conversation like I had a thousand times before. Who are you talking to these days? she asked casually, like tossing a stone into still water. I danced around that question too, giving just enough without giving away everything.

It had been my silent defense mechanism for years.

But that night, something was different. The air inside the car felt heavier, and the road seemed longer. And out of the quiet, she spoke words that shifted the entire night: "I had a dream last night that your friend wasn't a girl." I gripped the steering wheel a little tighter and kept my eyes forward.

Maybe if I didn't respond, the moment would pass. Perhaps if I stayed silent, I wouldn't have to answer. But respect and love demanded a response.

"What did you say?" I asked, trying to sound casual, though my heart was beating out of my chest. She repeated it, slower this time. "I had a dream that your friend wasn't a girl. Am I right?" And in that second, I realized something important: I had spent too much of my life giving partial truths. I watered myself down to make others more comfortable, living in a safe, edited version of my own story.

Not anymore. I took a breath that felt bigger than my body and said, "Yes. It's true." The world didn't end. The car didn't crash. She didn't turn away. Instead, she smiled—the kind of small, soft smile that parents give when they know their children have just handed them something fragile and sacred. And she said, "I love you no different."

No judgment.
No rejection.
Just love.

As the miles slipped by beneath our tires, she asked if she could meet "my friend." Not out of obligation. Not because she felt forced. But because she wanted to know the people who mattered to me—the real me.

And sitting in that car, under the dim glow of passing headlights, I realized: I had not just survived telling my truth; I had been embraced by it. That acceptance was powerful. It wrapped itself around me like a second skin—something earned, something sacred.

But deep down, I knew that not every space would echo the same grace that Aunt Grace and my mother had given. I understood there were still places where authenticity was dangerous, where truth could be wielded against you. And nowhere was that truth more vivid than within the four walls of the church.

* * *

It's sometimes amazing and heartbreaking how we can serve behind a mask. How you pour yourself into ministry, lift others, lead worship, and comfort broken hearts while hiding the parts of yourself that need comfort the most.

There's a strange, quiet violence that occurs when you are asked to be holy but not whole. When the very institution that preaches "come as you are" silently demands, but not like that.

I knew the rules. I had sensed the unspoken warnings long before I whispered my truth aloud.

There were certain topics you didn't bring to the altar. Certain struggles you buried beneath your Sunday best. Same-sex attraction wasn't just a sin to many—it was a scarlet letter, a brand that could strip away everything else good about you in their eyes.

And yet, despite all that, I loved. I loved fully. I fell deeply, madly, into a relationship with someone who made me laugh and knew how to quiet the storms inside my mind. After some conversations—and many late-night talks—we decided to step into the light, not just to love each other in the shadows, but to acknowledge it publicly.

It seemed so simple at first: a Facebook status update—one tiny change, one small act of courage.

It was a Friday afternoon. I had finished a long work week, my body tired but my spirit light. I sat at my desk, hovered over the "About Me" section, staring at that blank space that asked about relationships. I entered his name, paused, prayed, and then hit submit. It was posted in seconds. The world didn't end. The sky didn't fall.

Saturday came. Nothing. Sunday came. Stillness. Then came Monday: the firestorm.

OAKLAND HILLS, MILWAUKEE RIVERS

Whispers first—hushed conversations behind closed doors. Then comes the tidal wave. Phone calls. Messages. Eyes that once sparkled with warmth are now filled with something colder—something closer to pity or disgust.

Word traveled like wildfire, faster than truth could keep up—across cities, across states. And before I could catch my breath, I was no longer "Brother So-and-So" or "Faithful Servant."

I was a headline.
I was the whispered warning.
I was the cautionary tale.

The reactions in my local church fractured the community I once called family. Some stood by me, arms crossed over their chests in silent support, offering smiles that said, We love you anyway.

But others... others honed their tongues. Late-night meetings. Secret huddles. Special conversations designed not to seek understanding, but to plot my exit. I was no longer recognized for my years of service. For the hours dedicated to ministry. For the prayers, the sacrifices, and the support I had offered to others. No, all they perceived now was a sin they had deemed unforgivable.

It crushed me. The humiliation was raw, and the betrayal was bitter. It felt like being exiled from a home I had spent my whole life helping to build. This experience made me question deeply and painfully everything I believed I knew about unconditional love in faith communities.

For months, I carried that weight. Every Sunday service, every midweek Bible study, every moment walking through the church doors felt heavier and harder. It was a reminder: You can serve here, you can worship here, but you cannot be seen here in your entirety.

And yet... through it all, every whispered conversation and every sideways glance... Aunt Grace remained steady, unmoved, and unshaken. She called, hugged, and asked how I was holding up, but she never demanded that I explain or defend myself. She just loved me—loudly, publicly, without hesitation.

And through her actions, I was reminded: People might try to redefine your worth. Churches might try to edit your testimony. But love—the real kind, the love that covers and restores and redeems—doesn't flinch. It doesn't flee. It fights. In that season of rejection, Aunt Grace's love fought for me when I barely had the strength to fight for myself.

UNCONDITIONAL LOVE

There's something that most people don't tell you about heartbreak in the church: it's not just the people you lose; it's the version of yourself you thought you were building alongside them.

When the rejection came—slow at first, then roaring like a tidal wave—it didn't just take my sense of belonging. It shattered the foundation of where I thought my faith and community stood.

But here's the truth: *I didn't leave the church.*

I stayed.

I continued to show up, weekly, service after service, program after program. I remained in the same pews, worshiping alongside the same people who whispered about me in hidden corners. I kept serving, leading, and defending those who revealed my vulnerabilities through their careless words and secret conversations.

They don't always discuss the kind of spiritual trauma that develops in those spaces. It quietly erodes your sense of safety, trust in yourself, and understanding God's heart. I wrestled—not just with the people around me—but with the God I thought I knew.

For a long time, I wondered if perhaps I was the one who was wrong. If possibly loving the way I did meant I had somehow failed Him.

Late at night, those thoughts would creep in, uninvited. Was my love less pure? Were my prayers less powerful? Was my worship less accepted? Such questions make you question your place in the church and your place in the world.

And yet, even in the midst of that slow undoing, something inside me refused to die. Because somewhere beneath all the shame and second-guessing, a quieter truth was beginning to surface—one that had been there all along, waiting for me to notice it.

God created me entirely, not just the parts the church deemed acceptable or the aspects I had been taught to polish and present on Sunday mornings.

Every part—the parts that loved differently, laughed too loud, felt too deeply—had been crafted by His hands. Fearfully and wonderfully made. And because God created me, no human opinion, no whispered conversation, no judgmental glare, and no church meeting behind closed doors could redefine who I was.

Their rejection no longer dictated my identity, and their opinions no longer owned my peace. It took time because healing always does. But day by day, moment by moment, I began to rebuild. I realized my worth was never tied to anyone's comfort with my story. It was never about fitting into their fragile, fear-based interpretations of faith. It was about living the life God had called me to live—full, honest, and free.

And through it all, Aunt Grace remained steadfast. She didn't flinch, falter, look at me differently, or love me any less. Her love stood as a steady, immovable force—a mirror reflecting the kind of love I had almost forgotten existed. The kind that doesn't demand you shrink or ask you to choose between being loved and being known.

There will be seasons when the very places you once called safe feel anything but. When the hands that used to applaud you now point fingers. When the people you served turn away just when you need them most.

That's when life teaches you something fast: the greatest victory isn't in outrunning the storm—it's in standing firm within it, lifting your head high, and whispering to the world, and to yourself: *I'm still here. And I'm still worthy.*

CHAPTER 27
Highways and Interstates

"On some journeys, you will travel alone, and on others, you will have the blessing of having a partner."

Two and a half weeks off is long, especially when you're not used to slowing down. But I had worked too hard at that place to lose vacation days to the system. I counted the hours, did the math, and ensured every minute was accounted for. So, when the request was finally approved, a sense of relief washed over me. I was excited—not the giddy excitement, but the deep exhale kind, the peace that comes when you know rest is finally around the corner.

I had a plan: a road trip across the country. My frat brother, a full gas tank, a cooler of snacks, and the long stretch of interstate lay between me and my mom. But before I could taste that freedom or even map out the playlists and stops for gas station wings and roadside fruit stands, I had to tend to someone far more important—Aunt Grace.

Three things had always commanded my time: God, work, and Aunt Grace. They didn't rotate; they aligned. Each one was sacred and deserved sacrifice. Even on days when I didn't feel like it, even when the weight was heavy or the schedule was too tight, I never questioned it. Some obligations don't require reflection; they come from the soul.

OAKLAND HILLS, MILWAUKEE RIVERS

It was a Sunday. We had an afternoon service in Chicago at a guest church, the kind that welcomed us with foil-wrapped dinners after shouting for two hours straight. It wasn't unusual to find me somewhere between Milwaukee and Chicago on I-94 for ministry—Bible on the dash, gospel humming softly from the speakers. That stretch of highway was my second sanctuary. But this time was different.

I was doing it in Midnight—my brand-new 2010 Chevy Camaro this time.

She wasn't just a car; she was a manifestation—a promise fulfilled—my version of Bumblebee, the beloved Transformer. I told myself years ago that if I ever made it and had the money and means, I would buy that car. And I did. She was one of two Camaros in Milwaukee then, fresh off the production line, ordered, custom-picked, and delivered like a crown to a king.

Midnight was blacker than night, with burnt orange and black leather wrapping the interior like luxury and heat collided. The dashboard appeared to have been stitched by hand, each thread a symbol of precision. The LED lights glowed inside the doors, illuminating when I drove, casting a subtle hue that made the entire ride feel like something out of a movie. And it was mine. Paid for by discipline, hard work, and a few of Aunt Grace's financial lessons that still echoed in my head: "Always save something for a rainy day—even if it's five dollars. And always make sure you have good credit."

Those two gems had supported me.

I remember spinning out on the freeway in my old Monte Carlo. Shaken but unharmed, I decided it was time to trade up. So, I went to the dealership. And there it was—the book. The one with the models, the specs, and the trim packages. I flipped through it like a kid in a candy store. Then I saw it—the Camaro RS. I pointed. "That one."

We examined every detail: model, interior, and wheels. I handpicked it all. I chose my car like some people choose wedding rings. The race stripe came later—a burnt orange accent to ensure no one mistook my ride for another Camaro in town. In Milwaukee, especially back then, mistaken identity could cost you more than your pride. Therefore, I stood out on purpose. On principle.

And if anyone asked, I'd tell them: *"Aunt Grace's prayers cover me."*

That week, I told her I'd drive her to North Carolina. She had decided to move to be with Lydia and Edwin, her youngest daughter and son-in-law. It was bittersweet, but I understood. If there were two men Aunt Grace trusted outside her own children, it was me and Edwin. She made no secret of it. I was her "baby," her favorite. And Edwin? He was her bonus son—respectful, calm, a man who lived his vows like scripture.

I had watched him care for Lydia through some of the hardest times. His devotion and steadiness left an imprint on Aunt Grace and me. It was why she favored him and why I admired him. It's rare to see love expressed as service while still wrapped in gentleness. Edwin was a good dude; everybody knew it.

Lydia and Edwin had relocated for work, and Aunt Grace viewed it as a new chapter—an escape from the pain and pressure that had accumulated like dust in the corners of her Milwaukee life. Big Momma had passed, and something in Aunt Grace died too. Their houses—three in a row, lined up like sentinels on a block that once breathed community—no longer felt like home. The chain was broken, energy shifted, and laughter dulled.

And Aunt Grace... she carried on, as she always did. But you could see it in her eyes—she missed her mother. She missed feeling tethered.

The weight only grew heavier. As she aged, her body began to betray her, and so did the people she once protected. Intoxicated relatives brought chaos into the home. Money vanished from Bibles and medicine cabinets. I heard the stories. I saw the tears. I was there after the fights. I sat on the couch late into the night while she whispered truths too heavy for daylight.

She was tired. And so was I.

Then that Sunday night, after church, she called me.

"Hey, Granny," I said.

OAKLAND HILLS, MILWAUKEE RIVERS

"Hey, darling. Where are you?"

"On the highway, coming back from Chicago."

Silence.

Then: *"I'm tired and ready to go now."*

I blinked.

"Now?" I asked.

"Now!" she repeated, her voice firm, no hesitation.

"Yes, ma'am. I'll be there in an hour. I'm just going to stop by the house and change my clothes, and I'll be over to get you."

She didn't say anything else. Just hung up.

We were supposed to leave the next day, but one of my cousins—drunk, angry, violent—showed up and created yet another scene. His episodes were the kind that made you hold your breath: fighting, yelling, breaking things. Aunt Grace had reached her breaking point. That was it—the final straw.

When I pulled up, she was already outside—it was ten o'clock at night. She sat on the porch, fully dressed, rocking slowly. Her expression was a sermon—pain, resolve, fear, and faith all in one look.

She stood up as soon as she saw me. Her things were packed beside her. I didn't even have time to turn off the car before she headed toward the passenger side. My cousins had helped gather her bags, and we quickly loaded them into the trunk. Machines, meds, memory-filled boxes. Some, I'd learn later, also transported a few unwelcome roaches. But we didn't care. We were on a mission.

It would be a turnaround trip for me, so I packed light. However, Aunt Grace came prepared for a new life.

The night before, she and I had talked. She pulled out a yellow envelope—the kind used for mailing documents—inside which was $53,000—all cash.

She handed it to me.

HIGHWAYS AND INTERSTATES

"I want you to hold this package while I'm gone," she said. Anytime we heard the word "package," we knew it meant money. I opened the envelope and sat there counting it. She trusted me, but the last thing I wanted was for there to be any confusion about what was inside. I counted the bills individually, and we confirmed it: $53,000. I tore a piece of paper from the notebook beside her and tucked it into the envelope for reference.

I was speechless. It wasn't just money; it was her entire life savings, her safety net. And she gave it to me. No speech, no hesitation, just trust. I locked that envelope away in my safe when I got home and never spoke of it again. That was our secret, one I'd protect for her.

Before we left, she asked my godson to ride along. She didn't want me to drive back alone. He curled up in the back seat, snug beneath the covers, with a bag of food beside him. Aunt Grace always made sure there was food.

And so, we drove.

We had been on the road for hours. The hum of the tires became a kind of lullaby, steady and comforting, weaving itself between Aunt Grace's soft voice and the quiet rustle of my godson shifting in the back seat. Midnight glided down the highway like she was born for it—responsive, smooth, a low purr vibrating through the cabin as the miles slipped beneath us. The road just outside Louisville was open, wide, and inviting. Caught in the rhythm of her words and the warmth of our laughter, I let my foot push a little too heavily on the gas.

We were talking—just like always. Her voice, delicate yet deliberate, floated beside me like wind through a cracked window. She discussed her house, how life had changed, and what she desired for us all. Her words carried weight, but they also held purpose. I listened intently.

Then suddenly, a flicker of blue in the rearview mirror.

At first, it felt like a dream—a flash of light so subtle I blinked, unsure. But then came the unmistakable rotation of red and blue, a siren cry muffled by the Camaro's insulation, and the jolt of reality that yanked me out of the peace we had been cocooned in. I looked up again—this time more attentively—and there it was: a cruiser on my tail, lights dancing like fireworks against the early morning sky.

"Man…" I exhaled, jaw tight. I glanced at Aunt Grace, who calmly turned her head toward the window, no panic in her eyes—just a quiet concern, as if she had witnessed this story unfold before.

I eased Midnight over to the shoulder, her tires crunching against the gravel as we came to a stop. The silence inside the car was instant. My godson had awoken, peeking between the seats. Aunt Grace sat poised, her hands resting gently on her lap, waiting.

I saw the officer's silhouette through my side mirror. One step. Two. His hand rested on top of his holster. His flashlight flicked on, cutting through the morning dusk and illuminating the car's interior.

He stopped just short of my window.

Tap. Tap.

"License and registration," he said flatly, not unfriendly but not warm either—just business.

I slowly rolled down the window, handing him the documents. "Good morning, sir."

"Do you know why I pulled you over?"

I played the game. "No, sir, I don't."

He tilted his head slightly and glanced at the car—its sleek black frame gleaming even under the dim glow of the highway lamps.

"You were doing 13 miles over the limit. In a sports car that stands out," he said, with a slight smirk that didn't quite reach his eyes.

I nodded. "I understand."

He walked back to his cruiser without another word, and we sat in that stillness—Aunt Grace and I. The lights from the squad car cast shadows across the dashboard, blinking red, blue, red, blue, painting our faces in alternating hues of warning and worry.

I glanced at her, apologetic.

"You alright?" I asked.

She nodded gently. "Mm-hmm. Just be still."

The officer returned, ticket in hand.

"This is a citation for speeding—$150.10. You can pay it online or by mail. Slow down."

"Yes, sir," I said, taking the paper.

He walked away in silence.

The lights faded into the distance behind us as I pulled back onto the highway. The road stretched forward, dark and wide again, as if nothing had ever interrupted us. When I thought we might sit silently for a while, I heard her voice again—soft, amused, a little maternal.

"Alright now," she said, her tone seasoned with that familiar blend of concern and affection. "Slow down, baby. You don't need another ticket."

I laughed—a breath I didn't even know I was holding. That was Aunt Grace, always bringing light back into a tense moment. We settled back into conversation, the kind that could only happen on a road trip, between the lines, through the long hours, and with the wisdom of a woman who had seen too much to be rattled by a flashing light.

We rode on.

We finally made it to North Carolina just as the sky began to hint at morning—gray giving way to soft indigo, the darkness peeling back like a curtain. But long before we crossed the state line, the terrain had already started to change. We felt it first in the way the road climbed and curved, gently at first, then more insistently, as though it was leading us somewhere we needed to go but wanted us to earn it.

This wasn't just some backroad gravel path. No, this was the interstate—well-paved, developed, and stretching across the country like a concrete

OAKLAND HILLS, MILWAUKEE RIVERS

lifeline—but even well-laid highways couldn't smooth out the will of the mountains.

They rose around us like watchmen, silent and towering, their forested faces catching shadows and moonlight. The road carved through them—winding, elevated, and at times narrow enough to make you slow down and grip the wheel a little tighter. Guardrails hugged the edges, and we passed warning signs every few miles—*Caution: Steep Grade Ahead, Brake Check Area, Watch for Falling Rock*—reminders that even with all our engineering, nature still demanded our respect.

I glanced over at Aunt Grace. She sat quietly, her eyes fixed ahead, observing the lines of the road fade into the darkness.

The deeper we went, the more the fog settled in. It wasn't heavy, but it hovered—just low enough to make the distant hills look like soft mounds draped in linen. From certain bends in the road, you could see the valleys—vast and still, with specks of distant lights twinkling from homes nestled in the green. It was beautiful, but it also made you hold your breath. You didn't rush through these roads, not even in a Camaro.

The steepness wasn't sudden—it came in waves. One stretch felt like a calm rise, and then out of nowhere, the highway would dip or elevate again, making your ears pop slightly as you climbed higher. Trucks in the right lane rumbled slowly, their hazard lights blinking like tired eyes. Even Midnight, sleek and strong as she was, felt the resistance.

But we made it.

And once we cleared the final ridge and started descending, it felt like entering a new world. The trees thickened, the road leveled out, and the sky began to yawn open.

Aunt Grace perked up as we pulled into town despite the long ride. Although her body may have been weary, something in her spirit stood tall when she saw the house.

During the ride, she contacted Lydia and Edwin using her free prepaid phone, though ironically, she was on my phone plan. Still, she liked the idea of that little flip phone. Maybe it gave her a sense of control, a way to call someone when she wanted, without feeling dependent. She called and said, "We're here. We're down the street from the house. Come out."

And not moments later, there they stood.

Lydia and Edwin waited on the small porch, their silhouettes framed by the soft porch light. Lydia smiled with her arms crossed, while Edwin stood with his hands in his pockets, exuding that familiar quiet strength. Seeing them together felt like watching a lighthouse at the edge of a dark coast—steady, calm, and familiar.

The moment I parked, I could feel the difference in the atmosphere. The weight she had carried in Milwaukee didn't follow us here. Not fully. It lingered, yes, in memory. But the pressure? The heat of stress that had clung to her like humidity back home began to lift.

The first thing she noticed was the red dirt around the house's perimeter. It blanketed the ground like a desert rug, cracked in places and fine and soft in others. Aunt Grace smiled. She had grown up on this kind of earth—Southern soil—and it meant something to her. Maybe it reminded her of her roots, maybe it reminded her that she could still plant herself somewhere new.

I stepped out of the car and was immediately greeted by the sounds of the South: birds chirping overhead, cicadas buzzing their evening songs, and dragonflies slicing through the air in zigzagging patterns, like tiny helicopters with no clear destination. You could smell the pine, the fresh air, and the faint hint of wood smoke from a distant neighbor's chimney. And it was quiet. Still.

I opened her door and helped her out. She paused—not because she needed to—but because she wanted to. She took a slow breath, looked around, and then exhaled differently. This wasn't just catching her breath; this was letting go. This was relief.

Aunt Grace had escaped more than just a city. She had escaped heartbreak, betrayal, the sting of stolen money, the echoes of drunken shouting, and the loneliness of being surrounded by family who didn't know how to love her properly. Here, in this space with Edwin and Lydia, she could exhale. Here, she could be Grace—not Granny, momma, family ATM, or emotional sponge. Just Grace.

And this place—this humble home nestled among the trees and surrounded by red dirt—offered her that.

I visited North Carolina a few times while she was there. Each time, I knew where to find her. By the water. She always found it—whether a pond behind the house, a river curved around a park, or a tucked-away fish lake a few miles up the road. She'd often be there, convincing Lydia or Edwin to take her. Rod in hand, eyes on the ripple, spirit at rest. Fishing was never just a hobby for her. It was sacred. It was therapy. It was her prayer room.

Wherever there was water, there was Aunt Grace. She found peace in those waters. She reset. For a while, I think we all did. That lasted for several years. She stayed, settled, and established herself in that soil. Then, one day, she returned home.

I didn't understand why at the time. I couldn't wrap my head around her returning to a place that had hurt her so deeply. But now? Now, I do.

Because sometimes you leave not to escape forever but to heal. And once you've healed, the only thing left to do is return.

CHAPTER 28
Back Home

"There will come a moment when you walk away—to heal, to feel like yourself again. But sometimes, the very thing that made you leave will lead you right back to the place that once broke you."

It had been a few years since Aunt Grace left Milwaukee behind. She had traded its chaos for the quiet hills and slower pace of North Carolina, seeking sanctuary from the noise, the dysfunction, and the pain that once clung to her like wet clothes after a storm.

While she was away, I took on the quiet responsibility of caring for the house. It wasn't a request. It wasn't an obligation. It was a decision—a commitment. The house was left vacant when my cousin and her family moved to another state. And though Aunt Grace was gone, her house still breathed with the weight of her years. Letting it sit idle would have been financial quicksand. So, I stepped in with her early words echoing in my ears.

We didn't know how long she would stay in North Carolina, so I rented it out short-term—responsibility wrapped in necessity. Before that, though, the house needed to be cleared. I rallied my frat brothers—four solid men I could count on—and they showed up. It was a long, tiring day. I paid them—not because they asked, but because time is valuable, and friendship, though rich, shouldn't always come free.

That day, we uncovered more than just furniture and boxes. We uncovered decades. Memories were packed into every crawlspace, every closet, and every cabinet that groaned under the weight of things stored and forgotten. The basement was the crown jewel of chaos—floor to ceiling in some places, with relics of forty-plus years stacked like monuments. Upstairs wasn't much better. Drawers overflowed with mismatched lids and forgotten keepsakes. Even the crawl spaces held memories packed in dust. The garage groaned with boxes, furniture, and the emotional weight of a lifetime. Some things were hard to part with—photos, toys, and worn-out mementos. Others were just remnants of time: broken, rusted, and long untouched. Some things I told Aunt Grace about. Some, I didn't—for her peace, and mine.

I spent months renovating—new paint, carpet, and kitchen updates. Though once full of love and history, the house hadn't seen much renovation in decades. The walls carried the dull memory of outdated paint, and the floors creaked under the weight of years gone by. The kitchen, which once overflowed with the smells of Aunt Grace's home-cooked meals, now looked tired and faded—its linoleum peeling at the edges, the cabinets swollen from years of absorbing heat and moisture. And then there were the roaches—mostly harmless, but ever-present. They skittered across countertops and darted into crevices like shadows with legs, a quiet sign that the house hadn't had the movement or maintenance it once did. Aunt Grace hadn't been able to keep up with the cleaning like she used to. Her knees. Her back. Her breath. All of it slowed her down over the years. The mild infestation wasn't her fault—it was just another sign of how much life had changed.

It was hard work and cost me over $10,000, but if someone else was going to live in her space, it had to be right. Eventually, I found a tenant and managed rent collection, bills, and repairs while battling a mortgage company reluctant to transfer the deed. Being a property manager wasn't the plan, but I'd shoulder the load for Aunt Grace. She was worth it.

She never knew the whole story. I kept it that way. Life had handed her enough. Shielding her from the burden felt like repaying the years she protected others—this time, she got to be the one receiving.

Then one day, the phone rang. It was Aunt Grace, her voice soft and certain.

"I want to come back to my house!"

I paused, stunned but relieved. The tenant was late on rent again, and her lease was up—perfect timing. Now, it wouldn't be hard for me to tell her the lease wouldn't be renewed because the owner was moving back home.

I didn't hesitate.

"Okay," I told her. "I'll start working on it."

I had stored her belongings safely in the pod, which I'd been paying for since she left. I arranged its return like a long-lost piece of her soul finally coming home. The transition wasn't just logistical—it was spiritual. The house was waking up again.

A few months passed, and Aunt Grace was back home in Milwaukee. I managed to get everything in order for her without any major hiccups. When she moved back, she noticed that I had changed the house. The built-in cabinet in the living room was gone. The kitchen cabinets had all been replaced, with a new backsplash, updated appliances, and new countertops. She liked everything—except not having a pantry. I had hidden it to create more space and to finally move the refrigerator out of the middle of the kitchen floor. For Aunt Grace, that meant she couldn't stockpile food from the local pantries like she used to. For me, it was a strategy to keep the roaches from returning. Either way, she wasn't happy with that decision. Not long after, I noticed the refrigerator had returned to the center of the floor, and the pantry was slowly filling up with canned goods again.

Aunt Grace had battled a few health scares while in North Carolina, and every time, I showed up—without hesitation, without excuse. I didn't go because I had to; I went because I owed her. Not in the sense of burden, but in the deepest way love and loyalty can owe someone who shaped your life. She had given me so much growing up—love, protection, a safe place to land when the world was too hard. So now, when she needed someone, I was that person.

Through her knee replacement surgery, I sat beside her, sleeping upright in that unforgiving hospital chair just to be near. I watched monitors blink, answered when nurses called her name, and ensured she ate, even if it was just a few bites. I didn't think twice when she had to be transferred to Winston-Salem—an hour from where she lived—for more specialized care. I made the trip. I made every trip.

My job? They knew. They understood. I had sat down with my supervisor early on and explained everything—what Aunt Grace meant to me, the role she had played in my life, and why, if I ever needed to leave, it wouldn't be because I was trying to escape work but because I was being called to something greater. I had never called in sick, never had unplanned absences. I was reliable and consistent. So, when I said I needed to go, they knew it mattered.

She wasn't just my aunt—she was my heart's compass. The one who steered me when I was young and sheltered me during the storms I couldn't articulate. Being there for her wasn't an act of kindness—it was a sacred repayment. A divine echo of all the times she stood in the gap for me when I was a boy. Now, as a man, I stand in the gap for her.

When she returned to Milwaukee, she was different. She was more fragile, on oxygen more frequently, and her body moved more slowly. Her once vibrant steps through the kitchen had now turned into careful shuffles, guided by pain. Her holiday meals—those sweet potato pies and dressing—became instructions passed down while we cooked.

Her strength had shifted, and it broke me.

She never complained. Her faith carried her. Each time I asked how she was feeling, she responded with grace. "I'm feeling pretty well," she'd say even when the truth was buried under ten pills daily.

Her bladder infections, constant in NC, followed her home. We landed at St. Joseph's Hospital, again and again. Same place as the knee surgery. Same cold rooms. Same routine. But this time felt heavier. Her UTIs were more frequent and more painful. With each incident, her dignity suffered. Having to depend on others for assistance chipped away at her pride.

We tried to lighten it, catching her doing things she claimed she couldn't while teasing her with love. "Didn't you say you couldn't walk over there?" Laughter softened the edges and gave us all a little room to breathe.

But then came the diagnosis: declining kidney function. Her labs told a story her face was trying not to reveal. She had been pushing through the fatigue, swelling, and discomfort—things she rarely vocalized, but we noticed in her posture, deeper sighs, and the longer pauses between her sentences.

When the doctors mentioned dialysis, her face changed, not with fear, but with clear resistance. It was as if the mere mention of the word took something from her. The thought of being tethered to a machine multiple times a week—of living with a schedule dictated by tubes and lab numbers—was overwhelming. It wasn't living to her; it was surviving. And Aunt Grace wasn't meant just to survive.

She gazed at us, calm, resolved, and said, "I don't want that." Her voice didn't waver. There was no room for negotiation.

This wasn't a moment of hesitation; it was clarity. Her drawing a line was choosing quality of life over quantity of days. She had lived too freely, too fully, and too independently to spend her final chapters shackled to treatments she didn't believe in. Even in sickness, she demanded dignity.

We respected her wishes, not because we agreed with them or felt good about them, but because they were hers to make. Loving someone sometimes means letting them steer the ship, even when the waters are rough.

She stayed in the hospital longer than usual, and this time, the walls seemed to absorb her restlessness. St. Joseph's was a familiar place—its sterile white corridors and the rhythmic beeping of machines echoed memories from her past surgeries. But this stay felt heavier. It wasn't just her body that was tired; her spirit was, too.

Aunt Grace despised hospitals. She detested the way the gowns never quite fit, the food that was always bland and lukewarm, and how every hour felt like three. But most of all, she loathed the dependency. Having to press a button to request help and having to explain her pain repeatedly. It chipped away at her strength.

"I'm just tired," she'd whisper some days, not out of defeat, but from sheer emotional exhaustion.

The nurses were kind, but no nurse could replace her independence. Watching others assist her with tasks she once did effortlessly—pulling up her covers, helping her to the bathroom, arranging her pill trays—was a quiet humiliation for someone who had always stood alone.

Emotionally, it wore on her. There were times I'd find her staring out of the small hospital window, eyes glazed not with sadness, but with a far-off longing, as if she were somewhere else entirely. Maybe she was back in her kitchen, making sweet potato pie. Perhaps she was imagining the fish lake in North Carolina. Maybe she was remembering what it felt like to breathe without the hiss of oxygen beside her.

The visits came like clockwork—family and friends rotating in shifts. Her room was rarely empty. I'd walk in, and someone would walk out. We'd talk. We'd sit. We'd hold space. But all the attention couldn't silence the storm inside her. She smiled for us and prayed with us, but when night came, when the lights dimmed and the noise died down, she was left alone with her thoughts—and that's when it was hardest.

Ultimately, she returned home.

A hospital bed was delivered. Her oldest daughter moved in, taking the back room to assist with her care. However, even in her illness, Aunt Grace still found ways to look out for others. The house filled once more. The voices returned.

"Ma, do you need anything?" we'd ask.

Usually, the answer was no. Her room was packed wall to wall with things people had brought her over the years—comfort items, medical supplies, small shelves filled with snacks, bottled water, heating pads, pill organizers, and random gadgets she insisted on keeping within reach. The dresser top doubled as a medicine station, with her weekly pill packs next to a calendar, a Bible, and a few notepads filled with scribbled reminders. It wasn't clutter; it was command central. Every item served a purpose, and every space had a reason. It was her domain, a carefully built sanctuary of familiarity. Her room was a fortress of comfort and control in a world where both were slowly slipping away.

Still, she would call me. Groceries. Snacks. Cravings.

"Hello, darling, it's Momma. Give me a call, I need you to bring me…" she'd say. The list would follow. Then, sweetly, "I'll pay you when you get here. I love you."

She knew better. Her money was never good with me. If I had it, she had it.

I'd drop the items off, and without fail, it became a visit—two, sometimes three hours. Sometimes we watched TV. Sometimes she slept. I'd watch her sleep from the chair beside her bed, hands folded tightly in my lap, afraid my breath might disrupt her fragile rhythm. Her breathing had changed—deep, gasping inhales that expanded her chest almost violently, followed by abrupt, hollow exhales that seemed to drain her whole body. It wasn't the kind of breathing that lulled you into rest. It was the kind that made you sit upright, alert, every second ticking like thunder in your ears. I noticed it at the hospital and now at home.

It scared me.

I never showed it, not even in my posture. I'd sit in that chair, motionless, like a guard on duty. My eyes fixated on the rise and fall of her chest, studying it as if it held a secret. A secret I wasn't ready to uncover. Every pause felt like a cliffhanger—my heart quietly begged for the next inhale.

There were moments when I'd lean in to hear it. To make sure. To reassure myself that she was still with me. I didn't dare cry or even allow myself to think of the worst. I just watched. Making sure to hope and pray without words.

When she woke, our conversations picked up where we had left off. Work. Life. Love.

"You need somebody," she'd tell me. "Somebody to share this life with."

She always knew what was happening with me, especially after our talk. Her questions weren't idle curiosities; they were gentle nudges laced with care, coaxing me to open up. She never pushed, but somehow, she always knew when to ask. Whenever I came over to bring her a bag of snacks or something from the grocery store, she'd smile knowingly, as if she had called me not because she needed the items, but because she needed me.

Now I wonder—were those calls really about groceries? Or were they her way of saying, "*I miss you. Sit with me. I need to see your face. I need to feel that I'm not alone in this.*"

Maybe those voicemails weren't just reminders for Vienna sausages or a loaf of bread. Perhaps they were breadcrumbs she left me to follow—subtle signs of something deeper happening beneath the surface. Maybe she knew her time was drawing near, and those soft requests were her way of preparing me, holding on a little longer, and pulling me closer without alarming me.

Perhaps she understood what we did not.

Maybe she understood that sometimes, presence conveys what words never can.

Either way, when she called, I responded.

Always.

CHAPTER 29
Family Traditions

"Lessons are often wrapped in moments shared with those you love. They create memories you carry for a lifetime, leaving crumbs in your heart forever."

There were so many memories over the years. One Thanksgiving, I hosted the family at my house. I had bought a duplex several years prior and was proud to have accomplished something remarkable. Aunt Grace had always emphasized how important it was to have your own. After a few years of renting an apartment on the north side of Milwaukee, I knew it was time to invest in something I could call mine—something that represented a step forward. A place that gave me bragging rights not for ego, but for fulfillment.

Of all of us who had grown up in the house, I was considered Aunt Grace's favorite. I knew it. They knew it. And the family accepted it. But it wasn't the kind of favoritism that offered me special treatment or unlimited privileges. It was the kind that reassured her that the sacrifices she made weren't in vain. I tried my best to listen to her. I went to school, earned an education, and got a job that gave me the stability I always wanted. It wasn't physical labor like what she had endured, but it offered me the mental reward that the world doesn't always understand.

When I lived with Aunt Grace, she often told me to get an education and find a job that let me "slide around in a desk." It was her way of discouraging the hard labor that had defined her life. She shared stories of her days in the South—picking cotton with a sack in one hand and a baby in the other, just trying to carve out a living before she moved to Milwaukee. That grit, that sense of sacrifice, was woven into every lesson she imparted. And so, I listened.

That Thanksgiving, I wanted everything to be perfect. Everyone came over—Aunt Grace, Big Momma, my cousins, and even a few friends. I lived in the lower unit of the duplex and rented out the upper one, a move Aunt Grace had once advised me on. The food was a full spread—dressing, baked macaroni and cheese, collard greens, sweet potatoes, cornbread, fried catfish, chitterlings, black-eyed peas, pies, and cakes—everything you'd expect to see on a Southern holiday table. The aroma in the house was overwhelmingly good. Sweet cinnamon and nutmeg drifted from the sweet potatoes, tangling with the buttery scent of golden cornbread just pulled from the oven. The savory richness of the dressing filled the air like a blanket, layered with notes of sage, onion, bell pepper, celery, and love. You could smell the fried catfish crisping in oil and the unmistakable vinegar tang of collard greens simmering low on the stove. Even before a single bite, mouths watered, and stomachs growled. People kept peeking into the kitchen, asking how much longer it would be, fanning their faces from the heat but not daring to walk too far away. The scent alone made you feel like home had returned in full.

Aunt Grace taught me how to cook. I remember being in the kitchen as a child, her giving instructions, correcting me, and coaching me until the day it all stuck. She would point with her eyes, raise her eyebrows when I over-seasoned something, and whisper quiet affirmations when I got it right. In a Black household, people don't eat everybody's food, and they'll let you know in a heartbeat who made what. But that day, there were no side-eyes. No polite refusals. Everyone trusted my cooking, and that trust didn't come easily. I had earned it. Unlike a few others in the family whose dishes remained mysteriously untouched at past gatherings, my food was eaten confidently. That meant something. That meant everything.

FAMILY TRADITIONS

Before we took a bite of a holiday meal—especially on Thanksgiving or Christmas—it was tradition to look to the eldest in the room to offer wisdom and lead us in prayer. Our way was a quiet gesture of reverence, a sacred pause before the feast. That particular year, it was Big Momma's turn. She was nearing 80 then, small in stature—maybe 4'9" on a good day—with a head full of salt-and-pepper curls and cheeks that held a permanent rosy glow, just like Aunt Grace. But don't let her size fool you; what she lacked in height, she more than made up for in presence.

You felt it when Big Momma walked into a room before she said a word. Her respect wasn't demanded—it was earned, carried in the way she carried herself: firm, fearless, and full of wisdom from surviving things most of us couldn't name. However, it also came with fear—because you'd better not cross her. She'd threaten to shoot you, and the thing is, we all believed she meant it. But even in that fire, she carried a devotion to God. Church had always been a cornerstone in her life—that and her occasional beer. We loved her deeply, revered her, and knew better than to question her choices, even when they caught us off guard.

When I asked her to bless the meal, everyone gathered around the table with quiet anticipation. We joined hands, forming a circle of generations—little kids squirming in their seats, teenagers trying to look interested, adults already eyeing the food. Heads bowed, breaths held, waiting. But instead of a prayer, Big Momma opened her mouth and began to sing: "This little light of mine, I'm going to let it shine."

I looked up, startled. This wasn't what I expected. It wasn't what any of us expected. A few of my cousins exchanged glances—one let out a quiet laugh, while another raised their eyebrows, confused. Some kids giggled, unsure if they should be singing or remaining silent. Yet, no one interrupted. No one dared to stop her. Because no matter which generation you came from, there was an unspoken rule regarding Big Momma: you respected her, especially during her moments. And so, slowly, one by one, voices began to join in. Teenagers who had rolled their eyes moments earlier started to hum along. Adults picked up the melody. Even the littlest ones clapped in rhythm. The room, once filled with anticipation and a bit of confusion, transformed into something sacred. A spontaneous, holy moment—intergenerational harmony born out of reverence, surprise, and love.

It became one of those stories you carry in your bones, the kind that gets retold over and over, each time with a little more laughter and a little more awe. Aunt Grace usually hosted these gatherings, but didn't have to do so that year. She got to sit back, relax, and take it all in. For me, it was a proud moment—because I had the opportunity to honor her by stepping up and carrying a small part of the weight she had borne for so long.

CHAPTER 30
Transitions

"There will always come a time when the things that once covered you are no longer there, and in that moment, you must find the strength to stand on your own and navigate life."

For as long as I can remember, Aunt Grace has always been there—steady, vibrant, larger than life in the quiet ways that matter most. She is the constant thread woven through every season of my story—the one who covered me when others uncovered me, who saw me fully when others turned away.

But even the strongest threads and brightest lights eventually reach their final stretch. And nothing—not time, preparation, or even faith—can fully prepare your heart for the moment you realize the woman who helped shape your existence is slipping away.

The signs came slowly at first. She seemed a little more tired than usual, with a few more doctor's appointments and sighs, so she tried to hide behind her usual laughter. We all noticed but didn't want to name it yet. Naming it would make it real. For a while, we clung to the illusion that maybe, somehow, she would stay strong forever—perhaps the same strength that carried so many others would save her, too. But deep down, in the places we don't often talk about, we knew. Time was slipping away.

* * *

Aunt Grace's final hospital stay wasn't just a visit—it was a sign. I remember sitting in that sterile room, watching monitors beep rhythmically, trying to convince myself that she'd recover, that she always bounced back. But this time was different. Eventually, she was released from the hospital and came home, and we all knew we had to prepare—not just for what might come, but for what was already unfolding. We cleared the dining room entirely, removing the table, chairs, and everything else to make space for her hospital bed. It wasn't just a practical choice—it was symbolic. We were repositioning the center of the house to reflect who she had always been to us: the center of the family.

We didn't want her hidden behind a door, disconnected from the rhythm of the house. No, we wanted her where the sun could still kiss her skin, the aroma of prepared meals could drift her way, and the sound of conversation and laughter could remind her that life still pulsed around her. The dining room became sacred ground. Her hospital bed faced the front door and the kitchen, so she could see everyone who came and went—still watching over us, still present. The space took on a hush, a reverent stillness that fell over visitors as soon as they stepped inside.

Family and friends came in waves. Some stayed for minutes, while others lingered for hours. They sat gently on the edge of her bed or pulled chairs up close, as if gathering at the feet of a queen. They whispered prayers, shared stories, rubbed her hands, and expressed the feelings they had long kept in their hearts. There was an unspoken understanding that every visit might be the last. Even the youngest children, who typically raced through the house with reckless energy, hushed themselves in her presence. They gazed at her with wide eyes, sensing the moment's weight in ways they didn't yet have the words to articulate. Once filled with ordinary noise and motion, the house transformed into a sanctuary—a space where time slowed, and love enveloped every corner.

In that quiet, we also had to wrestle with the truth. We were saying goodbye in pieces. Every touch, every smile, every whispered "I love you" was an acknowledgment of what we knew was coming. There was no rushing this time and no pretending. Grief had already begun its slow approach, creeping in with every heavy breath she took. Yet still, in the middle of the sorrow, there was beauty. There was grace. And there was a collective determination to show up for her the way she had shown up for us all her life.

And Aunt Grace, even in those final months, remained herself—thoughtful, intentional, full of grace. She would get on the phone and call people. Not because she was lonely, but because she was checking in or reaching out. She'd ask how folks were doing, tell them to come by if they could, often asking them to bring her something like Vienna sausages, hog head cheese, or a Pepsi. In her own gentle way, she was making her rounds—making peace, making space, making sure no word was left unsaid. Every call felt like a thread being pulled into place, a stitch closing the final seams of her earthly work. In a sense, it was her farewell tour, but she didn't call it that. She just called it love. However, even in that moment, we weren't prepared. I wasn't prepared.

* * *

I had been traveling back and forth from Madison to Milwaukee, doing what I could—holding on to hope with each visit, praying silently that maybe this wasn't the end. Maybe Aunt Grace would defy the odds one more time, like she always did. But nothing—not the hospital visits, not the quiet tears, not even the subtle way her hand felt smaller in mine—could have prepared me for that call.

It was May 9, 2019, a date forever branded into my memory. One morning, the phone rang, and on the other end, I heard it: "Key Key, she's gone." Just like that. Three words that broke something inside me. My heart stopped—not figuratively, but in that literal, suspended way where time folds in on itself. I didn't cry right away. I couldn't. All I heard was hollering and screaming in the background. High-pitched, guttural, and uncontrollable. The kind of sound only grief makes when it catches you mid-breath. It wasn't just pain—it was regret. A sound of mourning laced with memory, layered with questions no one ever wants to ask: Did I love her enough? Did I honor her while she was here? Did we take her for granted?

That's the thing about people who give unconditional love. They give it so effortlessly that you sometimes forget they are not obligated to. Aunt Grace didn't love because it was easy—she loved because it was who she was. She poured into people who rarely poured back. She made room for mess, recovery, grace, and growth, even when others didn't always return the favor.

And I think, deep down, many of us didn't fully realize the magnitude of her presence until it was gone. Until her seat sat empty. Until the phone stopped ringing. Until the light she carried no longer cast shadows on our lives.

My relationship with her was sacred. She trusted me with things that extended beyond the practical. One of those things was her life insurance policy. She made me the beneficiary, not because of favoritism, but because she believed in me. She trusted that I would honor her life, values, and wishes. And I wanted to. I needed to. But even with that clarity of purpose, the responsibility was overwhelming. By this time, I had already navigated loss—Big Momma, my father—but this was different. This was Aunt Grace. My guide. My steady. My compass. And now, I had to be strong again, but this time... for everyone else.

There's something uniquely cruel and sacred about being the "strong one" in the family. Everyone looks to you for the answers, coordination, and calm in the chaos. But they don't always see the cracks beneath the surface—the part of you that's breaking while holding everyone else together. This invisible weight settles onto your shoulders like something you never put on, but somehow always wear. You don't complain. You just carry it. Because somewhere along the way, your love for that person becomes the fuel that pushes you forward.

I often wonder if I've ever truly made peace with it all: losing her and having to lead the charge while my heart quietly shattered. I think the circumstances of my childhood—being separated from my biological parents—prepared me to compartmentalize pain in ways I still don't fully understand. When you grow up learning not to expect permanence, you teach yourself how not to feel certain things too deeply. It's a defense mechanism, but it comes at a cost. You learn to move on quickly and show up even when your heart isn't in one piece. And that's what I did.

Aunt Grace's passing wasn't just a family loss—it was a spiritual shift. Her transition shook the core of who we were as a unit. Yet, while mourning, I had to organize, plan, and arrange. I needed to ensure the world knew who she was and why she mattered. People came from every corner of the city and beyond to appreciate her life initially. However, I knew that her celebration wouldn't just be about flowers and programs, but preserving the legacy of a woman who had stitched this family together with wisdom, forgiveness, and faith.

In that season, I became both the mourner and the minister, the grieving soul and the keeper of order, the child who lost a mother figure and the man who had to stand tall so others could lean on him. And in that space, between heartbreak and honor, I discovered that sometimes the strongest way to love someone is to carry their legacy when their voice can no longer speak.

After she passed, everything slowed—but not enough for me to grieve. The world doesn't pause when you lose someone you love; it just hands you a checklist. A cold, emotionless list of tasks must be completed, even while your heart breaks. I had to ensure the arrangements were made. There was no waiting. The first call I had to make was to the funeral home to have her body picked up. That sentence still feels wrong—*her body*. Because even though I knew she had transitioned, my mind refused to separate the physical from the spiritual. That was Aunt Grace. That was my anchor. And now I had to speak of her in the past tense and treat her like an item on a to-do list.

I called the church where she attended to ask for availability, for service preferences, and for what options remained. The founding pastor had passed away a couple of years ago, and now a new pastor was leading the church. It all felt so clinical. I was making plans for someone I still wished I could call on the phone.

Writing the obituary was one of the hardest things I've ever done. Every word felt like a goodbye I wasn't ready to say. The pictures, the sayings, the memories. You find yourself trying to fit a lifetime into a few paragraphs, capturing someone who meant everything in a few neat lines that would sit under their photo in a program. As you write, the memories come rushing in through her laugh, her sayings, and how she'd enter a room and shift its temperature with just her presence. You think about the time she stood up for you when no one else did, how she cooked your favorite meal without you ever asking, and how she looked at you with eyes that said, "I see you." Somewhere between remembering and writing, the grief hits you all over again. Because you realize this is the last time you'll ever get to speak for her—the last story you'll ever tell with her in it.

What people don't understand—what they can't know unless they've lived it—is the emotional cost of managing arrangements for someone who raised you, supported you, and loved you unconditionally. Everyone else sees the coordination. They see the strong one making phone calls, organizing the details, and ensuring everyone is on the same page. What they don't see is the private collapse that occurs between tasks. The way your breath catches when you say her name. The lump in your throat when the funeral home asks what color dress she should wear. The tears that fall silently in the car after visiting the florist or the cemetery. And they certainly don't see the toll of trying to be the glue for everyone else while you're barely holding yourself together.

I had to pick out flowers—not just what looked nice, but what felt like her. Elegant. Strong. Timeless. Something that honored the life she lived and the legacy she left behind. Then there was the burial plot. That part was oddly grounding. Aunt Grace and I had talked about it many times. She didn't want to leave us guessing. We had already chosen the site and had begun making the payments. Still, it felt surreal when it came time to go with her children to finalize everything. We stood at the cemetery, walking the grounds, speaking to the manager as if we were ordering something off a menu—plot locations, headstone options, and remaining balances. But underneath all the planning was a heavy truth none of us could say: This is real. This is happening. She's not coming back.

And yet, I carried on because I had to. Because she trusted me. Because being her beneficiary wasn't just about insurance—it was about stewardship and carrying out her final wishes with dignity, detail, and love. It was about making sure her transition felt like the sacred passing of a queen, not the quiet fading of someone forgotten.

Planning her funeral meant living in memory while carrying the burden of reality. It meant smiling through phone calls while breaking down in private. It meant juggling sympathy from others while holding back your own emotions. And above all, it meant coming to terms with the fact that the person who gave you so much would never walk through your door again, call your phone, or say "I'm proud of you" one more time. That reality hurt me more than anything.

But I moved forward. Aunt Grace didn't just teach me how to live—she taught me how to lead. In that moment, I had to lead the family, guiding them through the fog of grief and ensuring that every step we took honored the woman who had carried us for so long.

* * *

We finally finished the planning process and were ready to celebrate her life. People had come to pay their respects during the visitation period at the church—old coworkers, family members, neighborhood friends, and relatives from far and wide. We were all dressed in purple accents, her favorite color, as a tribute to her life. She had purple carpet in her bedroom, and we felt it was only fitting to honor her as she transitioned in life. The sanctuary glowed with shades of purple—lapels, scarves, and flower arrangements. It was more than a color; it was her presence enveloping us like a royal embrace.

That day felt different. It was heavy before it even began. The kind of day when time drags, and your emotions have no rhythm—where grief and gratitude take turns leading your heart. We were at her home church, where her voice had once lifted in praise, her hands had clapped in testimony, her spirit had worshipped without restraint, and her tithes and offerings were sent. Yet, even this sacred space felt altered. The current pastor didn't have a personal relationship with Aunt Grace—she had been sick for years and wasn't as present at church. Once again, I needed to make a decision—another responsibility to carry. While planning the services, I reached out to my own pastor, a man who had known Aunt Grace since he was a kid, and asked him to deliver the eulogy. It was a choice made with prayer, care, and the full weight of knowing this moment would never happen again.

One by one, people stood and made their way to the microphone. The service had begun. The hush of reverence was met with stories, laughter, and tear-soaked reflections. They spoke about her cooking—how she could get folks to bring her food with just a hint of suggestion. They joked about how you couldn't tell her "No," especially if she used her soft, sweet, and mesmerizing voice. Someone talked about how she'd sit on her porch and wave at every single person who passed by, whether she knew them or not, and how she always had something to give: food, advice, a kind word, or just the comfort of her presence.

Then came the fishing stories. Multiple people shared how Aunt Grace could get you out on that lake before you even realized you had agreed. She had a way of gathering folks—on the water, in the kitchen, at church—and making them feel like they belonged. Whether it was with a rod and reel or a Sunday dinner, Aunt Grace reeled people in with love. She sacrificed more than people knew, giving until it hurt and never complaining. She mothered generations, many not biologically hers, who always called her "mom." And even in her discipline, she was gentle. She corrected you with a look, guided you with a sigh, and covered you with a prayer.

The church held all of that. All of her. And there she was—laid to rest in a white casket with silver accents that shimmered under the soft sanctuary lights. It was regal, dignified, and gentle—just like her. The casket's interior, above her head, featured a custom graphic with her face, smiling peacefully, and a scripture that reminded all of us of her unwavering faith. As people walked slowly by to view her body, the air seemed to hold its breath.

She looked absolutely beautiful, resting in perfect peace, dressed in a crisp purple dress and a white scarf that wrapped delicately across her neck. It was the color she loved most, and in that moment, it crowned her one last time. Her hair was perfectly styled in the tight curls she had always favored, framing her face like a halo. She looked like royalty—like the queen she had always been to us. There was something almost celestial about the way she lay there, still and serene, as though even death itself knew to tread softly around her.

People paused, hands over hearts, some in quiet prayer, others unable to hold back their tears. The hush that fell over the room wasn't just grief—it was reverence. We weren't just saying goodbye; we were acknowledging the presence of a woman who had shaped generations with her love, wisdom, and grace. She looked untouched by suffering, glowing instead with a sense of eternal rest. Her body may have been still, but her spirit was alive in every tear, every hymn, and every memory that flooded the room. Until the moment came: the song.

When "I Shall Wear a Crown" began, something shifted. You could feel the atmosphere break. It wasn't just a song—it was a declaration. A sacred testimony that her journey, her labor, and her sacrifices were not in vain. As the soloist opened his mouth, playing on that digital piano, the first note soared across the sanctuary and pierced every guarded heart in the room. The words wrapped around us, pouring into the cracks left by her absence. People wept openly—deep, wrenching sobs that filled the space like incense. Some lifted their hands, some rocked in their seats, some whispered "thank you, Lord" under trembling breaths. It was the kind of moment only the Black church understands—where song becomes intercession, where melody becomes memory, where grief and glory intertwine.

In that moment, Aunt Grace was with us—crowned not just in heaven, but in the hearts of all who loved her. The weight she carried now rests on those she shaped. And I knew, deep in my soul, I would carry it forward—with purpose, not performance.

Because that's what she would have done. And because that's what her grace taught me to do.

CHAPTER 31
The Conclusion

"Nothing happens without purpose. Life comforts, teaches, and builds us through lessons to strengthen our testimony to help someone else along the journey."

This is the book's conclusion, but it is not the end. As I write this chapter, I can't help but reflect on how this quietly mirrors a pivotal age in life where I embraced my truth. And somehow, it feels fitting. This chapter feels less like a closing and more like a rebirth—a quiet awakening into a life no longer bound by silence, fear, or pain. A life no longer shaped only by what happened to me or what people thought of me, but by what grew out of it.

I carried stories I didn't know how to tell for much of my life. But in these pages, I found the courage to speak. In honoring Aunt Grace, I found freedom. Her love didn't just lift me; it gave me purpose. Through every challenge I faced, every loss I endured, and every chapter I lived, I began to realize that none of it—absolutely none of it—was without meaning. Everything served a purpose. Every tear. Every setback. Every unanswered question. They were all teaching tools, building blocks. Now, those lessons live as testimony.

THE CONCLUSION

Aunt Grace saw aspects of myself I had yet to discover. Through her care, I found glimpses of the person I could become.

However, she was not the only one.

My father taught me about presence and absence in his imperfections and humanity. In the moments when he showed up and when he didn't, I learned the importance of being there for myself. His transition left a space that forced me to evaluate forgiveness, legacy, and the kind of man I wanted to be. My mother, in her complexity, gave me life and truth. Our journey was not without struggle, but it was ours. Through her, I learned what it means to carry both gratitude and grief—and how love can exist in complicated spaces.

And then there were others—like my ex-girlfriend—who held mirrors up to my wounds. Love, in that space, was both healing and a teacher. Through our relationship, I learned vulnerability. I learned that healing doesn't always come from being understood, but from understanding yourself in the aftermath. Loving and losing her taught me that some connections are seasonal, but the lessons can last a lifetime.

Each of these people, every friend, every relative, every conflict, every reconciliation—served a divine purpose. They all shaped the path that led me here. They chipped away at the parts of me that were still hiding. They added color to the portrait of my identity. And when I look at the man I am today—a higher education leader, a storyteller, a son, a protector of legacy—I see not just one influence, but many. I see the fingerprints of everyone who ever touched my life, especially those who loved me enough to help me grow.

I have stood at the crossroads of what was and what had to be. I've stood in quiet hospital rooms, in crowded church pews, in empty apartments, and on brightly lit stages. I've stood as a boy searching for answers, and now I stand as a man charged with carrying the legacy of those who gave everything so I could thrive. And through it all, Aunt Grace—whether physically beside me or spiritually within me—has remained the thread that ties every version of myself together.

OAKLAND HILLS, MILWAUKEE RIVERS

This book began as a memoir, a personal story. But as I wrote, revisiting the corners of my childhood in Oakland and the complexities of my life in Milwaukee, it became clear that this wasn't just about me. This was about the people who supported me, lifted me, and loved me through brokenness and brilliance. Ultimately, this book became about Aunt Grace.

She didn't enter my life by accident. She arrived with a purpose. And like the very best gifts, she gave herself fully and quietly. There was no announcement, no grand display—just a woman with a heart big enough to hold a fractured boy and a spirit strong enough to raise him into a man. She didn't just house me; she healed me in ways I didn't understand until much later.

She taught me that strength is often silent. That you can bear the weight of the world and still prepare dinner, still press clothes, still whisper prayers at night over children who have no idea how many battles you've already fought for them. She was the matriarch, yes—but more than that, she was the quiet architect of my resilience. I owe much of who I am today to the foundation she built with weary hands and an unwavering heart.

Her wisdom is embedded in how I lead. Every student I mentor reflects that influence. In the policy I shape, her influence echoes quietly. She didn't just guide my life—she left fingerprints on everything I now touch.

But losing her shattered me in ways I struggle to articulate. You can prepare the flowers, write the obituary, and arrange the burial plot—but nothing prepares you for the moment you realize the voice that once called your name in comfort will never call it again. That the hands that once held your trembling fingers now lie still. That's the one who always knew how to find you, even when lost, won't be there to find you the next time.

And yet, in the quiet of that absence, something miraculous happens: you begin to hear them differently. Not in sound, but in soul. You hear them in your choices, your courage, and your compassion. Aunt Grace still speaks to me. Every time I choose patience over pride, love over judgment, and faith over fear, she is there.

THE CONCLUSION

This journey—Oakland Hills, Milwaukee Rivers—has always been about navigating life's unpredictable currents: the split between two worlds, the lessons etched in loss and love. But now, with this second edition, it also becomes a testimony to the people who shaped the journey. Aunt Grace was not just part of my story—she was the soul of it.

So, to every reader: I hope you found yourself somewhere in these pages. I hope you see your own Aunt Grace, or Big Momma, or father, or cousin, or neighbor—someone who covered you before you knew how to cover yourself. Someone who taught you how to stand.

Life happens to all of us, but it never occurs without purpose. What once hurt us has shaped us, and what once felt like the end has become our beginning.

This signifies my rebirth.

This is the chapter where silence no longer binds me, secrets no longer define me, and grief no longer holds me hostage. This is where I step into the man I have always been becoming.

Everything I've become and am becoming results from her always loving and living with me. She fulfilled her purpose not through fame, but through love. I am her living testimony—every step I take now is part of her legacy.

This was therapy. This was healing. This was forgiveness. But most importantly, this marked the end of what was and the beginning of what is.

But even as I stood in that moment—grateful, whole, forgiven—there was still one part of my truth I hadn't spoken. Not to the church. Not to my family. Not even to myself in full. A part that didn't fit neatly into healing circles or altar calls. It lived beneath the surface, the Sunday best, and the polished testimony. And as much as I wanted to leave it buried, I knew I couldn't close this story without opening *that* door. Not the one tied to survival—but the one bound to desire. To control. To curiosity. To the kind of silence that doesn't scream, but lingers.

And what happened next?

I've never said it out loud—until now.

EPILOGUE
Unresolved Thoughts

"Some things we don't confess with words. We confess through choices, by bodies, and through silence."

Oakland wasn't the only thing I returned to. There was something about being back in California—the air, the rhythm, the ghosts—that stirred parts of me I thought I had outgrown. Old emotions started whispering again. Some soft. Some sharp. I told myself I was there for family, healing, and reconnecting with my mother. And that was true. But it wasn't the whole truth.

The other truth was quieter. More complicated. It wasn't packed in my suitcase, but I carried it all the same.

It had been a long day—tense smiles, awkward laughs, and that particular kind of exhaustion that only comes when you're pretending everything's fine. I sat on the edge of the hotel bed, scrolling through my phone. Not looking for trouble. Just… something that didn't require translation.

That's when I opened Jack'd.

He didn't ask for much. His profile was simple. No thirst traps. Just a clean headshot and a couple of sentences that told me he wasn't here to play games. We chatted for a little while, and I noticed he had a calm, curious energy in his messages that made it easy to respond. Feeling comfortable, I gave him my hotel address and room number.

No deep conversation.

No expectations.

No overthinking.

I wasn't looking for anything serious. I was visiting anyway, and there was no way to bring *this* back with me to Wisconsin.

And maybe that's what I needed most. Not a chase. Not a commitment. Just a space where I didn't have to explain the weight I was carrying.

* * *

The knock on the door came twenty minutes later.

I opened it—and froze.

I thought to myself, "Damn! He looks better in person." That was sometimes common feedback I'd receive from the guys back at home. However, having it reversed now was what I needed. There he stood—tall, with smooth brown skin that glowed under the hallway light, a trimmed beard framing his jawline, and a simple chain resting just below the collarbone of his hoodie. His build was strong but not showy, as if he was confident without trying to be. His eyes were kind. Steady. And something about how he looked at me suggested he knew I wasn't just letting him into the room. I was letting him into a part of me I had spent years trying to silence.

"Hey," he said.

I stepped aside to let him in. The door clicked shut behind him, and for a moment, it felt like the outside world had been locked out—and maybe, just maybe, a part of myself had been locked in.

He stood at the edge of the bed, scanning the room before turning to face me again.

No awkwardness.

OAKLAND HILLS, MILWAUKEE RIVERS

No posturing.

Just presence.

Calm and comfortable, he waited for my lead. That moment—his quiet confidence, his lack of demand—brought up something unexpected.

* * *

I had flown into California on another attempt to rebuild things with my mother. She was trying, and I was trying. But trying doesn't always translate into healing. We still had work to do.

My father was gone, not just dead, but absent long before death arrived. He was absent from the years he should've shown up, from the lessons he never taught, and from the manhood I had to figure out alone.

I didn't talk about it much anymore after he passed, but it still spoke—just in different ways.

Tonight, it spoke through silence, through invitation, and through the comfort of a man who didn't ask for a version of me I had to rehearse.

* * *

He peeled off his hoodie and laid it across the chair. His arms were toned, with soft tattoos curling along his forearms like script only he could read. He didn't take up space in the room; he fit into it. Like water in a vessel, his energy met me where I was.

I motioned toward the bed.

He followed.

No playlist hummed in the background. No fake laughter filled the air. Just the sounds of breathing and closeness.

And in that stillness, I allowed myself to feel.

He reached out first, fingers tracing the curve of my chest, then pausing as if to ask a question without words. I didn't speak. I didn't flinch. I answered by remaining still.

It wasn't wild. It wasn't urgent. It was careful. Intentional. Like two people discovering something they weren't sure they had permission to want—but needed anyway.

Afterward, we lay in silence. He rested on his back, one arm stretched behind his head, the other across his stomach. His eyes traced the ceiling, like he was reading his own thoughts quietly.

"You good?" he asked.

I nodded. "Yeah."

But that wasn't the full truth. I didn't do this because I was "good." I did it because I was tired of waiting to be chosen. Tired of molding myself into spaces that were never shaped for me. Tired of performing healing in public while still feeling fragmented in private. And tired of the church praying away a part of me I never asked to be prayed over.

This wasn't about craving a man. It was about reclaiming a part I had been taught to fear.

When he left, I stood by the window, watching the glow of headlights weave through the city below. I didn't feel guilty. I didn't feel heroic. I just felt… real. And sometimes, real is all you're trying to be when the world keeps asking you to shrink.

* * *

I used to think that coming out meant the hiding would stop. But hiding doesn't always look like fear. Sometimes, it looks like control. Sometimes, it looks like hotel rooms, short answers, and intimacy, which you script in your favor because you're afraid of losing again.

Some of you might still be asking: *So… is he gay?*

A question many often wonder: you spend a lifetime loving women, being intimate with them, being raised by them, and admiring their beauty, both inwardly and outwardly. Then this?

However, the question you ask is the wrong question.

OAKLAND HILLS, MILWAUKEE RIVERS

Try this instead:

Can you still be whole while your story is unfolding?

Because that night wasn't about a label. It was about liberation. It represented a version of me that stopped asking for permission and lived—even if only for a night.

This isn't the end of my story. It's just the part I never thought I'd say aloud. But I'm ready now. There's more—so much more. About ache. About appetite. About acceptance. About forgiveness.

You've walked through my hills. You've crossed my rivers.

But next...you'll meet my reflection in the ***Mirrors***.

Stay with me.

Acknowledgments

Up until this point, I have never felt such immense joy and excitement in creating something that I could share with the world—a token of my unwavering commitment and a testament to the daunting experiences that have shaped me. This work serves as a demonstration that every challenge, every moment of doubt, was worth it in the end. As the beginning of what I hope will be many contributions, I would be remiss if I didn't acknowledge the incredible support I have received, making this body of work possible.

I must first thank my mom, Doris. Your journey inspires me in ways that are sometimes beyond words. It's often unfathomable to witness how strong, brave, caring, unique, and loving you are as a mother. There is no doubt in my mind that you love me deeply and want nothing but the best for me. You alone have given me the strength and courage to write this book. Thank you for accepting me wholeheartedly, regardless of the nontraditional paths or decisions I make daily.

To my late Aunt Mercie, there isn't a day that goes by when I don't miss your presence here on earth. I know God created you to help guide me, and for that, I am forever grateful. Every lesson you taught me, every hug you gave, and every moment of unconditional love you shared have left an indelible mark on my life. Nothing went unnoticed, and my life has been a testament to showing you just how thankful I am. I believe you would be proud of me for what we have accomplished together. To my Aunt Carolyn, thank you for always having so much pride in who I've become and for never hesitating to amplify and celebrate my accomplishments—especially as "the Doctor." Your unwavering support in everything I do and your drive, determination, and business acumen have inspired me to pursue every idea that comes to mind with confidence and tenacity.

To my village—Demetrius, Shaun, Corey, Martell, Maria, Elicia, Denita, Traci, and Schunn—thank you for always supporting me and my endeavors. Your friendship means the world to me. Knowing how excited you were about my book fueled my determination and confirmed that this is exactly what I was meant to do. God, kids, I love all 30 of y'all—do something remarkable!

I extend my deepest gratitude to those who have served as role models and impactful leaders in my life. To Bishop Gregory L. Goner, I appreciate our conversations and the invaluable opportunity to observe you in your leadership element. Those interactions have greatly strengthened my confidence, and I have learned so much from you.

To my work colleagues who have shown me kindness and support, thank you. Tracey—thank you for being willing to read my work first. Your insights and feedback mean so much and have enhanced the passion I poured into this project. And to Debbie, thank you for always being there, for your willingness to help, and for your cherished friendship. You embody what it means to be a true friend, and I treasure that deeply.

To everyone who has ever shared or commented on one of my Facebook posts, retweeted my messages, or reached out to me asking for KeyWORDS—thank you. Your public and private encouragement has been instrumental in shaping the ideas that ultimately launched this book. It has taken time to get here, but your engagement and belief in my words have played a vital role in bringing this vision to life. Finally, to Brandyne, thank you for taking the time to go through all of my posts to extract everything I've shared online. To all who read these pages, I hope you are inspired by the stories and messages captured here. It is my deepest desire that this work

ACKNOWLEDGMENTS

resonates with you and ignites a sense of hope, purpose, and strength. Thank you for being part of this journey.

About the Author

Dr. Keyimani L. Alford is an accomplished leader, educator, and author whose life revolves around inspiring others and creating opportunities for growth and transformation. With over two decades of experience in leadership roles across diverse industries, Dr. Alford brings a unique blend of professional expertise, personal resilience, and unwavering dedication to his craft. His journey from humble beginnings to becoming a published author and respected leader is a testament to the power of perseverance, self-discovery, and authenticity.

Dr. Alford's professional career encompasses higher education, enrollment management, and student success. He has held influential roles in institutions of higher learning, where he has been instrumental in designing and implementing programs that promote equity, inclusion, and student achievement. Renowned for his innovative thinking and results-driven leadership, Dr. Alford has spearheaded initiatives to increase access to education for underrepresented populations, enhance retention rates, and create supportive learning environments for all students. His commitment

ABOUT THE AUTHOR

to excellence and his ability to inspire those around him have established him as a trusted mentor, colleague, and advocate for change.

As a lifelong learner, Dr. Alford holds a Doctor of Education (Ph.D.), which he pursued to deepen his understanding of leadership and its role in shaping institutional and societal transformation. His educational journey reflects his belief in the transformative power of knowledge and his commitment to personal and professional growth. Dr. Alford's passion for learning is evident in his academic achievements and his continuous efforts to expand his skills and perspectives, which he applies to every aspect of his work and writing.

As an author, Dr. Alford shares his life story and insights in his debut book, Oakland Hills, Milwaukee Rivers. This deeply personal memoir chronicles his experiences growing up in Oakland, California, and Milwaukee, Wisconsin, navigating the challenges of family separation, societal expectations, and self-doubt. Through vivid storytelling, Dr. Alford reflects on the pivotal moments that shaped him and the lessons he learned along the way. The book is not only a reflection of his personal journey but also serves as a source of inspiration for readers seeking to overcome their own challenges and embrace their unique path.

Beyond his professional achievements, Dr. Alford is passionate about storytelling, mentorship, and community building. Through his platform KeyWORDS, he shares impactful quotes and messages designed to inspire hope, resilience, and self-discovery. His work is driven by a desire to empower others to find their voice, recognize their potential, and trust in the process of growth and transformation.

Dr. Alford's story is one of resilience, purpose, and the belief that every challenge provides growth opportunities. Through his leadership, writing, or speaking, he continues to inspire individuals and communities to embrace their journeys and create meaningful change. Oakland Hills, Milwaukee Rivers reflects his mission to connect, uplift, and transform lives, one story at a time.

Other Publications
by Keyimani Alford

Available at www.drkeyspeaks.com

www.ingramcontent.com/pod-product-compliance
Lightning Source LLC
Chambersburg PA
CBHW030454100526
44580CB00010B/133/J